GROWING UP MUSLIM IN AMERICA

Stories by Muslim Youth

By Youth Communication

Edited by Marie Glancy O'Shea

Growing Up MUSLIM in America

Executive Editors
Keith Hefner and Laura Longhine

Contributing Editors
Tamar Rothenberg, Alexandra Ringe, Philip Kay, Clarence Haynes, Katia Hetter, Nora McCarthy, Autumn Spanne, and Hope Vanderberg

Layout & Design
Efrain Reyes, Jr. and Jeff Faerber

Cover Art
YC Art Dept.

For reprint information, please contact Youth Communication.

ISBN 978-1-935552-38-3

Second, Expanded Edition

Printed in the United States of America

Youth Communication®
New York, New York
www.youthcomm.org

Catalog Item #YD36-1

Table of Contents

Using the Book

Introduction

For Muslim teens living in America, life is unavoidably political. What other young people may see as purely personal questions of self-expression—how to dress, whether to date, what music to listen to—Muslim teens often experience as a wrenching choice between religion, tradition, and family on the one hand, and peers and American identity on the other. This was the case even before September 11, 2001, but since then their situation has grown more complex. Widespread stereotypes reinforced by media, not to mention new immigration and security policies, have helped create an atmosphere of mutual distrust. For teenagers trying to understand who they are and where they belong, that atmosphere is especially confusing.

In this book, teens from Muslim backgrounds write about what it means to be both Muslim and American. They write about their religious faith, and what it takes to express that faith in a country where it's not the norm. For one thing, it takes guts: "I was expecting my friends to come over to me, asking why I was wearing it ... but they didn't even talk to me," writes Maria Zaman of the day she debuted her hijab, or head scarf, in school. It also takes self-control, as Abanty Farzana found out when she started to be interested in boys. "It seemed that all my classmates were dating while I wasn't," she writes, adding, "I didn't like feeling left out, but I also didn't want to defy my parents." She admits that not dating continues to be a challenge, but she's heartened to find a sympathetic ear in her mother.

Other writers focus on the parts of American culture they've embraced. Isma Aslam celebrates her love for indie rock music, and Zeba Khann explains why she's happy to surrender her claim on any identity other than American. "The so-called American culture is more than blue jeans, hot dogs, and apple pie," Zeba writes. "It's a feeling that lets us know that no matter how different we are, we have at least two common bonds: our pride in being American, and our ability to communicate with each other effectively."

These bonds, though, don't shield Muslim-American teens from the prejudice and outright aggression they sometimes face. As a young Lebanese male traveling in the early 1990s (shortly after the first attack on the World Trade Center) Mohamad Bazzi is treated with suspicion on reentering the U.S. Years later, 9/11 would cause suspicion to simmer over into hostility. Writing in the weeks after the tragedy, several teens in this book express their hurt and anger at being blamed for acts they consider abhorrent.

They also describe their fear. After Sara Said's life is threatened on her way to school, she feels an urge to return to the Middle East, where she will be guaranteed acceptance as an Arab Muslim. "I didn't want to live someplace where every day I walked in the streets feeling like an alien in fear of being attacked," she writes. But instead of hiding, Sara combats ignorance with information; she and two Muslim peers organize a conference at her school to educate classmates about Islam.

Other writers who have moved to the U.S. from Muslim countries have special reasons to be glad of their relocation. Mohammad Ali belongs to a Kurdish family that made a harrowing escape from Saddam Hussein's Iraq; though their lives in New York are far from perfect, Mohammad and his father value the political stability of the United States. Sarvenaz Ezzati, who with her mother fled her overbearing father and the oppression of women in Ayatollah Khoemeini's Iran, has no doubt about where she'd rather be: "I know that I could never live like the many Iranian women who take orders from their husbands and are financially and socially dependent," she writes. Orubba Almansouri is also grateful for the educational opportunities she found in the U.S., but feels torn between ambition and obedience. Unwilling to disobey her father, she lives in hope that he will allow her to go to college; in her dark moments she worries her American-born dreams have been for nothing.

Many forces work on a Muslim teen in America, suggesting who she is and who she should be. Among these are parents and family, religion and traditional culture, school and friends, media, and even strangers on the street. Making sense of so many influences is not simple or easy, but through writing, the teens published here register their own voices in the conversation. We hope they inspire other teens to do the same.

Karolina Zaniesienko

Holding On to Who I Am

By Zaineb Nadeem

When I was 12, my family and I moved to the United States from Faisalabad, Pakistan. My parents brought me and my two brothers here so that we could go to American schools and colleges.

Two days after we arrived, my mother told me something I'd never heard her say in Pakistan: "Always remember who you are and never be afraid of people talking about you."

My father added, "People from different countries live here and they might criticize you for your looks and language, but remember who you are and speak up if you feel you have to. Try to be a confident girl."

I remember listening to them with my eyes down. I didn't know what they were talking about.

Back in Pakistan, everyone around me looked the same and believed the same things. I didn't understand how much my culture made me who I am. And I didn't understand that I would have to make sacrifices to hold on to my identity in my new home. But I started to learn as soon as I entered my first American classroom.

On my first day of school, I had a big smile on my face as I walked into my 8th grade class. I was expecting to make lots of friends, just as I had in Pakistan.

I didn't think twice about my clothes. I was wearing what I'd worn all my life, the traditional dress for females in Pakistan: a loose, long shirt ending a little above my knees; pants, and a long scarf around my neck. All of my body was covered except my head, neck, and hands. In Islam, a girl is supposed to hide her body so men don't think of her as their property. You only show your body to the person you're going to marry.

As I entered the class I noticed that there were black and white students, but no Pakistani kids. Lots of the girls were wearing jeans and short tops. No one was dressed like me.

I was scared. This was the first time in my life anyone had talked to me about sex directly.

For the first week, I smiled and said "Hi" to everybody I knew from my class. They said "Hi" back, but with a smile that seemed unfriendly and strange. They stared at my clothes, looking at me from top to bottom. I wanted to hide.

About three weeks later, I was sitting at a cafeteria table apart from everybody. A black girl sat down, asked me my name and then asked, "Why do you wear this dress in school?"

"It is my cultural dress," I replied.

She told me I should change the way I dress. I didn't know much English at the time (my native language is Urdu), so I didn't ask why. But I started to think that if I changed my way of dressing, that girl and I might become friends.

I considered talking it out with my mom, but I knew my parents would be very hurt if they saw me changing to be like the other kids. My family's love was more important to me than having friends just for the time I spent in school. So I accepted feeling lonely.

Luckily, after about five weeks, I left that school because my family moved. My new middle school was an international school with students from China, Russia, Bangladesh, and other countries, including Pakistan. I was excited to meet people from my country. I thought I would be more comfortable with them and we would understand each other.

Soon I became friends with a group of seven Pakistani girls from my class. They were good students. I wanted to be part of their group because they seemed to share my goal to get the most out of school. My new friends dressed in American clothes. There were other Pakistani girls who wore traditional clothes, but I wasn't as eager to be in their group because they didn't pay attention in class.

My friendship with the studious Pakistani girls happened easily. We started sitting together at lunch and walking together on the playground. I talked to them about movies, songs, and school, just like I'd talked to my friends back in Pakistan.

But from the beginning, we were also different. My friends talked to each other about dating, and I felt a little uncomfortable knowing that they were going against our culture's beliefs. We don't date or have sex before marriage. But since they weren't trying to include me in those conversations, I didn't let it bother me much.

Then, after a few months, one of my friends came up to me after school and started talking about a guy she'd recently gone on a date with. She told me, "We are planning to have sex."

When I heard this, and when she started to describe hugging and kissing her boyfriend, I was scared. This was the first time in my life anyone had talked to me about sex directly. In Muslim houses, sex isn't discussed in front of children, because it's believed that it will seduce them into having it. So when she began talking, all I wanted was for her to stop. I was afraid I would be seduced into having sex. Even if I wasn't, I was afraid talking about it might have a bad effect on my reputation, and I was afraid somehow my mom would find out that I was talking about sex.

But I didn't want to upset my friend by saying that I thought it was wrong to date and have sex. Plus, according to my culture, it's her family's duty, not a friend's, to tell her what is wrong and what is right. So instead, I tried to change the topic by talking about history class. When she kept on talking about sex, I left, saying that I needed to see my teacher for extra help.

It wasn't long until other friends also began talking to me openly about sex. I tried to avoid the subject. I felt more and more uncomfortable with them. I didn't want other Pakistani students, my teachers who were from my country, or my parents to think that I was like these girls. I started to wish I had friends who didn't date and were more like me.

Then, one day toward the end of the school year, one of my friends spoke up about my clothes during lunch. She started telling me that now that I was in America, I should change the way I dress and speak.

"You're like an old-fashioned girl, wearing this dress and speaking Urdu. I think you should start dressing the way we dress," she said. I still remember how her voice sounded, mean and nasty.

My other friends agreed with her. I was angry because my clothes and language are part of me, so when they told me to change them, I felt they were trying to change my inner self. Suddenly, I didn't feel like eating anything. A storm was building inside me. I heard my mother's voice in my head saying, "Be confident. Say what you want to say."

"I will stay the way I am," I said. "Are we friends only if we dress alike? I love my culture, and I won't change at any cost."

They just made fun, saying, "You talk like an old woman." I hated them for saying this to me. I felt really low and lonely because they were more interested in my dress and language than in me.

I wasn't going to be friends with people who weren't going to accept me. For the first time since I'd come to the U.S., I'd declared my pride in my culture. I felt more sure of who I was than ever before. But I also felt like an alien, and lonely.

A week after that, I was sitting alone when a Pakistani girl in traditional dress came up to me and started a conversation. The next day she greeted me again, and from then on we started sitting together at lunch.

I'd declared my pride in my culture. I felt sure of who I was. But I felt like an alien.

We talked about schoolwork, and I found that she was a good student. I started going to her house, something I hadn't done with my other friends. She asked me why I left my other friends and I told her the story. She agreed with what I'd done. She, too, is determined to follow our cultural traditions. We became best friends.

I'm now 17, and these days I have friends from other cultures. We have fun together doing after school activities like yearbook committee and student government. I enjoy talking to them about our classes and about music, movies, and books. Sometimes we talk about our cultures' traditional foods and dress, and sometimes we discuss our cultures' beliefs about sex and dating. I'm more comfortable talking about sex now because we've studied it in school and I'm used to the topic.

I still don't want to date before I get married, and I still don't want to hear the details of other people's personal relationships. I like knowing that when I'm married, I'll belong only to one person who will also belong only to me, and that only the two of us will know about our intimacy.

But I respect the way my friends from other cultures choose to live their lives—I don't want to change them, just as they aren't trying to change me. The conversations we have are respectful and comfortable, and nobody tries to make fun of someone else's values, the way my old group of friends did with me.

I've learned that I'm most comfortable around people who share my basic cultural and religious beliefs. Just as my family understands me, my pride in my identity, and the choices I've made to hold on to that identity, I want my closest friends to understand these things, too.

Zaineb was 16 when she wrote this story.

Cezary Ladocha

Jidda's Strength, Courage, and Wisdom

By Sara Said

"No, NO! I don't want to put any oil or henna on my hair!" I cried. I was 9, and still living in Yemen. My grandmother—my mother's mother—sat there trying to convince me that I should always put henna and oil on my hair.

I hated how olive oil made my hair all slippery. And I hated how henna made my hair and fingers turn reddish.

But I knew that even if I complained, I'd have henna on my hair somehow. Sometimes I'd wake up from a nap and feel my hair oily and full of henna; my grandma knew I slept like the dead and would seize the opportunity to put henna on me.

Even though it made me a little mad, it also made me laugh. And it reminded me of how much I admired my grandma for her strong will and wisdom. My grandma—who I call Jidda, which means "Grandma" in Arabic—is in charge of making decisions in my mother's family. When she talks, my uncles and aunts listen to her quietly.

It was my grandmother who told my mother how to care for my siblings and me when we were ill. She knew how to give us medicine when we refused. "It's juice," she'd say, handing it to us in a regular cup. "It will make you strong."

But when I was 10, I moved with my mother and siblings to America, where my father had gone when I was 6. I cried about leaving Jidda. Her eyes turned into tears that day, too. Her tears still remain in my heart. It's been six years since I've seen her.

Even though she didn't know how to read, she had wisdom.

Now we talk on the phone about once a month. "Assalam Alaikum," I greet my grandmother when one of my parents hands me the phone. "How are you?"

I tell her about school and how much I miss her. I hold tightly to the phone, trying to catch Jidda's words.

Taking a moment, she'll say, "I am fine, praise be to God," as if trying to sound like she's in great health. She always tells me that what makes her happy is hearing the echoes of our voices. When I hear her voice, I feel happy too, but scared that it'll be the last I'll hear from her. Jidda's not in good health; she has cancer.

I worry that some day soon I'll come home from school and get the news that she's passed away, and that makes me feel depressed. I feel hopeless not being able to do anything to help her in her illness.

But despite her health now, when I think of Jidda, I think of her strength. I admire her a lot for the strength that she has inside her and the great faith that she has in God.

I felt her strength in the stories she used to tell us about growing up in a village in Yemen. My siblings and I used to sit around her in a circle, like a kindergarten class, our senses alive as we listened to our Jidda.

Jidda told us stories about the difficulties she faced growing up. Her family wasn't able to send her to school because there were no schools in her village at that time. My grandma never learned to read, but she did memorize surahs (or chapters) from the Qur'an to help her pray. Even though she didn't know how to read, she had wisdom to help her in life and to pass on to her children.

In the village, there weren't many jobs other than farm work. In her teenage years, she had to work hard in order to help her mom and the rest of her family. She grew crops and took care of her other siblings.

To me, my Jidda's hands were a symbol of her hardship. They looked tired and rough. Her skin is dark and I remember how I could see her veins popping out of her skin.

My grandmother used to wake up at 4 or 5 a.m. to pray and then get water from the river with other women carrying buckets on their heads. One time, when they set out for the river in the afternoon, the women misjudged the time and almost got caught in the dark. It wasn't safe to be outside at night; that's when dangerous animals came out. So they turned back to go home.

But as they were walking, they saw a leopard standing about 25 feet away! Everyone was scared and, as my grandmother told us, they all made funny sounds. Jidda kept hushing them, saying "Shh, shh." The way my Jidda told the story made me feel she wasn't scared.

The women had a lamp so they could see where they were going. However, Jidda realized that the leopard was looking at the lamp, so she turned it off. Then she and the others ran quietly behind a huge rock so the leopard wouldn't see them.

When the women were behind the rock, she told them, "I don't want to hear any voices coming from you. If any of you make any sound, I will throw you out to the leopard." She was serious and all of them were scared—of the leopard, and of my grandma.

Then, Jidda told us, she realized that the leopard was trying to smell their scent. So she tried to think of something that would distract it. In the darkness of the night, she ran quietly and swiftly to a certain distance. Trying to distract the leopard, she turned on the lamp. As the animal caught the gleaming light, she ran the other way and led the women to the farm.

I remember thinking how brave my Jidda was. Looking back, I think she told us the story because she probably wanted us to never fear anything. My grandma must have been scared when she saw the leopard. Who wouldn't be? But she couldn't show it or admit it to herself because that would just make her feel more scared. Instead, she stayed calm and concentrated on what she had to do.

In my life, too, there have been times when I've needed to be brave. After the tragedy of Sept. 11, as an Arab Muslim, I was in constant fear that someone would hurt me or my family because of who we are. But I had to stay brave like my beloved grandma and stand up to my fears. I told myself out loud, "I fear no one but God."

All of them were scared—of the leopard, and of my grandma.

Jidda always says that God is watching over her and us. She always looks at the positive side of things, and says that everything will be all right if a person makes the right decision and has faith in God and one's self.

I admire Jidda's spiritual strength. Like her, I get my optimism from prayer and listening to recitations of the Qur'an. Singing about the prophets and listening to Islamic songs on the Internet helps me when I'm feeling down.

I hope I become a strong woman like my grandma. I miss everything about her. Her voice still echoes in my ears as I think of her, though it sounds tired even in my mind, as if she's struggling to speak clearly.

I can still remember the smell of my grandmother, like henna and herbs. And while I still avoid putting henna on my hair, I like using it for traditional decorations on my hands. When I do, I tell my sister, "Smell the henna! It reminds me of grandma." I inhale deeply and say into the air, "I miss you, Jidda."

Sara was 16 when she wrote this story. She later graduated from Brooklyn College with a degree in secondary education and history.

My Love Affair With Indie Music

By Isma Aslam

"I don't have any of that type of music. This is all I have," I told my cousin as he searched through my iPod looking for Bollywood music.

"Yeah, didn't you know?" my brother asked my cousin. "She only listens to white music."

"It's not white music," I said, angrily. "And why would I listen to Bollywood music? I can barely understand the language without subtitles. You know that."

I felt the weight of my brother and my cousin staring at me. "I'm sorry, but it's what I like!" I said.

To my friends and family, I'm pint-sized, pessimistic, no confidence, sarcastic, and worried Isma. I'm also religious Isma—praying, teaching children how to read the Qur'an, and practicing my own recital of the Qur'an throughout the day.

But I'm also Isma, the alternative and indie rock music junkie.

I blame my love affair on a boy. I walked into class on the first day of high school four years ago and immediately noticed a blond head with spiky hair. He stood out, and not just because he was the only white student in the classroom. (I stood out as much as he did, with a black scarf covering my head.)

It was clear that he was a rocker not only by his band shirt, but by the numerous band patches stitched onto his backpack. He was also definitely a looker, and I was drawn to him. I'd been a pop music fan, but that day signaled the end of my pop music days and the start of something new.

I don't initiate conversation with strangers, let alone a boy I think is cute. So how would I find out anything about him? Luckily, I became friends with a Goth girl named Terica who spoke quite a bit to this boy. Most of the time I'd hear them arguing about music, so I listened (without making it obvious) in case he named a specific band.

I'm religious Isma—praying, teaching children how to read the Qur'an. But I'm also Isma, the indie rock music junkie.

Sometimes during their discussions Terica would ask me to come to her defense. I had no idea what was going on, but I'd nod my head and pretend to be in the know. When I worked up the nerve to ask Terica about him, she said, "He's a punk."

"Punk? What's punk?" I wondered to myself. Terica explained that he listened to punk rock music, a sub-genre of rock music. I went home and downloaded some punk after researching a few artists off the Internet, and boy, I did not like it!

I couldn't find anything appealing about loud music and barely audible lyrics. That didn't cut it as music to me. But I was disgustingly lovesick so I thought I could start off with some of punk's softer and more comprehensible music.

I stumbled upon pop punk, which incorporates elements of

pop and punk rock music. It's feel-good type music with rock band instruments and mostly understandable lyrics. I began listening to artists like The All-American Rejects and the very early music of Brand New. I actually liked this music. I loved how it was one step closer to my goal, but still close to my own taste.

Terica gradually noticed a shift in me; she was surprised that I was listening to this band or even knew about that band. As far as I was concerned, I was still the same Isma, with just a minor alteration in my musical tastes. But my interest took root. After two years of longing for the blond boy, I just stopped finding him attractive. Yet I found myself as attracted to alternative rock music as ever.

Terica fed my addiction by giving me my first alternative album, *Where You Want to Be*, by Taking Back Sunday. I loved it. Gradually, I moved from only pop punk to other types of alternative music. Without even realizing it, I was thoroughly enjoying punk rock, general alternative rock, and progressive rock. Much to my shock, I actually started hating the pop music I once loved. It seemed so childish and not my type of music anymore.

Now, lying in bed at night, I listen to one particular song by Brand New that's played in the most beautifully sad way. The last verse starts, "This is the end/This story's old but it goes on and on until we disappear/This is the calm/Calm me and let me taste the salt you breathed while you were underneath.../ You know that you are not alone/I need you like water in my lungs."

I'm filled with serenity listening to those few lines. The lyrics are sad, yet peaceful. The way the vocalist sings them makes me feel that much closer to the song and to him. Sometimes I swear I can actually feel him singing the words. Now that's a sign of inspirational writing (and perhaps a loss of sanity on my part).

I respect and admire the lyrics that Brand New vocalist Jesse Lacey composes. The writing is so beautiful that it inspires me to become a good writer, to write something that inspires someone.

And now I want to learn how to play guitar. I always wanted to play piano, until a friend of mine suggested bass guitar. Isma plus bass guitar equals questionable, even laughable. But why not? As if me falling in love with alternative rock music weren't shocking enough!

Four years later, Terica is aware of my music addiction, but most of my other friends still aren't. I can't blame them—it's not like I've shared this part of me with them. But I recently started sharing a bit, since I'm considering taking up guitar in college and I feel I need to state my influences.

Isma plus bass guitar equals questionable, even laughable. But why not?

What's been incredible about my evolution is how music has become a constant in my life. For the past four years, there hasn't been a time when I've been without music. Except for the moments when I obviously can't play music—in the shower, at work, in class—I always have it turned on.

I wasn't even this crazy during my boy band days—and I loved my boy bands! Indie music has made me more defined and inspired. I'm always excited to see which of my bands has a new release so I can rush out and buy the album. And I'm always trying to interpret some of my favorite lyrics by Brand New. I have an addiction that I don't wish to break free of.

Isma was 18 when she wrote this story.
She went on to attend Vassar College.

Living Single: As a Muslim, I Don't Date

By Abanty Farzana

As a Muslim teenager, I find myself having to explain a lot of my beliefs and traditions to non-Muslims, particularly when it comes to dating. Because of religious tradition, most practicing Muslims don't date. That comes as a shock to many American teenagers because they tend to fixate on romantic love and relationships.

The truth is that, growing up as a teenager in America, it's been hard at times to accept the Muslim traditions myself. Not dating makes me different from most of my classmates. I don't have much of a life other than school, work, and hanging out with friends. On weekends, I usually hang out with my family, which includes not only my brother and parents, but also my cousins, aunts, and uncles.

We're Bangladeshi. In our culture, families tend to be close;

like mine, many get together almost every weekend, so that takes up time. I don't know how I'd fit in time for a love life, even if I could have one.

It's not written in the Qur'an that Muslims aren't allowed to date, but it's implied, and that's what our elders teach us. Boys and girls are allowed to be friends. But the closeness of the friendship has its limits. If it reaches a point where it could almost be romantic, then it's considered wrong. That's why many Muslim parents don't allow their children to have too much interaction with members of the opposite sex.

Adults don't date either. Many Muslims who go to college marry in their early to mid-20s, after they graduate. And yes, many have arranged marriages, a concept that I realize many people think is weird. "How do you not date?" they ask. "What, you can't pick who you're gonna marry?"

In junior high, I had major crushes on boys. I didn't understand why I couldn't date.

All the marriages in my family were arranged, and they have worked out. Maybe that's just a coincidence and many couples aren't as lucky. But the couples I know seem happy and committed.

My parents were classmates in college before they got married. They liked each other and were friends, but it was their parents who decided they should get married. My aunt and uncle only met each other once before their wedding, when he went with relatives to her house. They both agreed to the match. Both of these are good working marriages.

But I understand why the idea of arranged marriages may seem unreal and confusing to non-Muslims. In junior high, I had major crushes on boys. I constantly tried to talk to them in hopes of becoming friends, and I didn't understand why I couldn't date.

All I understood was my parents' attitude toward American forms of romance. When we saw couples kissing outside, they'd say "We don't do that"—meaning Muslims don't show public displays of affection. If there was kissing on TV, they'd change the channel.

My parents didn't like me watching TV shows that featured teen romance, so I was stuck watching kiddie shows like Barney when I was 13. When I turned to a channel that depicted romance, they made me change it or told me that I shouldn't watch those shows.

But I snuck to the TV sometimes and watched *Beverly Hills 90210* anyway.

By the time I turned 14, it seemed that all my classmates were dating. Since I wasn't, I felt I didn't have much to talk about with my friends and classmates. Dating seemed like a "normal" part of a teen's life to me.

At the same time, because I was surrounded by dating I worried that my parents thought I was doing it, too. I didn't talk a lot about my friends or my life in school with my parents and I worried that they thought I was hiding something. I felt guilty trying to watch the romantic TV shows that they didn't approve of.

Looking back, I think my fears that they didn't trust me had more to do with my own doubts about whether I could trust myself to be obedient. I didn't like feeling left out, but I also didn't want to defy my parents.

A couple of months into my freshman year, my mother realized that I had something on my mind. "Abanty, what's wrong?" she began.

I was reluctant to answer. But she saw right through me.

"Why are you sad lately?" she asked. "Did you do badly on a test? Or did you have a fight with friends?"

"I just have a lot on my mind," I told her. But I opened up a little, and somehow we worked our way around to the topic of dating without mentioning it straightforwardly. We sat in the kitchen for some time discussing how tough it is to live in America as a Muslim teenager.

"I know it seems that everyone else has different experiences than you and it makes you feel left out," my mother said. She continued, "I was a depressed teenager. I got upset and overwhelmed myself with the smallest things until I talked to someone about it and realized that others have the same problems." It was a relief to feel like my mother understood.

I have some Muslim friends whose parents worry so much about their children dating that they hold onto them with a tight leash. One Muslim girl I know got in trouble for sneaking around with her boyfriend. Her parents found out and forced her not to see him again, but she kept seeing him and ended up getting caught once more. She finally ended the relationship, but her parents are now reluctant to trust her and are even more overprotective.

Being a Muslim teen who hides a relationship from her family would be doubly difficult.

I'm thankful to my parents for allowing me to be independent, yet giving me rules to follow and support. They don't believe that constantly forcing a child to follow her parents' rules is the best way to get the child to listen and obey. They even realized that the TV shows I like to watch had little effect on me and they gave me more freedom to watch them. My parents find that encouragement and support are more positive parental influences than too many rules.

Though I was unhappy freshman year about not being able to date, I gradually decided that my friends were as much as I could handle socially. Many of my friends who date complain about how it takes up too much of their time, or they get annoyed with the person they're seeing. I like not having to deal with that. Not dating has kept me more focused on things I want to do with my life right now, like writing and working hard in school.

Also, my parents' trust is very important to me. I don't want to disappoint them by being a disobedient daughter, and I haven't found someone I consider worth getting into that much trouble for this early in my life. Being a Muslim teenager in America is complicated enough. Having to be a Muslim teen who hides a relationship from her family, including her own parents, would be doubly difficult.

Still, not dating is hard. Most of my friends who don't date, Muslim or otherwise, are sometimes saddened by being alone. I think relationships, whether friendly or romantic, are part of a teenager's life, and without experiencing the latter, I sometimes feel like I'm missing out.

These days, when I start feeling that way I usually talk to my cousins. They have to deal with the same situation, so it doesn't feel weird when we talk to each other about it. My friends are sympathetic, but most of them can't relate to my situation.

I'm hoping that if I can survive through high school without giving into the pressure of dating, I should be able to make it through college, too. I'll probably start thinking about meeting a guy to marry around the time of my college graduation. Thinking about it now makes me laugh, because I don't feel ready to go through that process. I don't know whether or not I'll have an arranged marriage, though it's a strong possibility; I have to wait and see.

I realize that if I go away to college and I'm not living at home, it may be tougher to maintain my non-dating stand. But I know that I'm level-headed enough to do what's best for me. Maybe I'm being Little Ms. Goody-Goody, but if refraining from dating leaves me without any regrets, then that's what's right for me. And if I can stay true to my parents and my religion while being self-reliant, then that's even better.

Abanty was 16 when she wrote this story. She went on to attend Temple University, where she majored in journalism.

YC Art Dept.

Where's Your Bomb?

By Mohamad Bazzi

Some people imagine it's exciting to be an immigrant. I've learned to shrug them off. I tell them if they think it's so much fun, they should try going through immigration and customs inspections at Kennedy Airport—in my shoes.

My Lebanese passport makes airport officials nervous. Not only am I Lebanese but I'm a Muslim, and even worse, I'm a Shiite. I'm also a young man, so they assume the worst: I must be a religious fanatic waiting to blow up a plane.

"Where's that bomb?" they probably ask themselves. "Come on, kid. Don't waste our time."

Last year I was coming back from visiting my brother who lives in Paris when an official saw my documents and pulled me aside. His colleague asked where I had been. "Paris," I said.

"What were you doing there?" he shot back, as if the concept of a Lebanese immigrant vacationing in Paris defied all logic. I explained, but he still seemed skeptical.

"Do you have anything in there that you shouldn't be carrying?" he asked, pointing to the suitcase.

"Like what?" I asked innocently.

"I don't know. You tell me."

"I don't think so," I answered, unsure if it was a trap.

"Well, let's just check," he said, instructing me to open my bags. So unlike most other travelers (especially American passport holders, who were getting a warm welcome and breezing right through), I had my bags rummaged through, once again.

My Lebanese passport makes airport officials nervous.

In a way, I felt violated. Why me? Should I get an American passport and change my name from Mohamad to Michael so that I can get through the inspection more quickly?

These customs agents are America's way of welcoming its immigrants. It doesn't sound as good as your textbooks make it out to be, does it? No Statue of Liberty on the horizon; no fireworks—just lots of questions and dirty looks.

Mohamad was 17 when he wrote this story. He went on to graduate from the City University of New York and became the Middle East Bureau Chief for Newsday. *He is currently a professor of journalism at NYU.*

Showing My Faith on the Outside

By Maria Zaman

Instead of my mom's usual chatter, all I heard in the car on the way to school that October morning was the DJ. "Now some more hit songs!"

I could just feel the tension in the air. I was in the 6th grade, and for the first time, I was wearing the hijab to school. It's a headscarf worn by Muslim girls and women that covers the hair, neck, ears, and shoulders.

When we arrived at the schoolyard, Mom said, "Maria, you're making a big decision here. I really don't want you going ahead with this. I know you're going to be treated as an outcast. No one's going to want you to be their friend. Come on, no one's forcing you to do this." I could hear the pleading in her voice.

Out of 24 students in my class, there were four Asians, one

Hispanic, and one Pakistani—me. The rest were white. My mom was worried that I would stand out by wearing the hijab.

With a heavy heart, I said, "Mom, I know there's no pressure. I'm doing this for Allah, and for him only."

Her face fell, and she went quiet for a moment. I felt guilty. I'd never wanted to make her so upset.

"What can I say to that?" she said in a flat, defeated tone. Her comment stung because I wanted her support. And she wasn't the only one who disapproved. I'd talked to my older cousins Salma and Uzma in England, and they said that I was too young to wear the hijab, that I didn't know what I was getting into.

I felt alone in my decision, but determined. I got out of the car and walked into school, thinking I could handle whatever happened with God's help. I didn't know how hard it would be.

When I was growing up, my family wasn't too religious. My mom had never worn the hijab, nor had anyone in my immediate family or my first cousins. (Mom told me that she'd been raised in a sheltered community of Muslims in England, where the hijab wasn't needed because everyone respected each other and modesty was the norm.)

I wanted to get even closer to God, so I decided to wear the hijab all the time.

My family and I did the basic Muslim things, like fasting during Ramadan, giving zakaat (charity), and celebrating Eid (a Muslim holiday). We also ate halal meat, which is meat from animals that have been killed according to the rules of Islam. Yet we didn't do some important things, such as praying the five daily prayers Muslims traditionally say.

Like other Muslim parents, my mom and dad sent me to religious education classes at our mosque and to duhrst, or discussion groups held at people's houses where girls talk about Islam and society. From a young age, I loved learning about Islam and Allah—I wanted to know everything about my faith and live by it.

As was customary, I wore the hijab to my mosque and to duhrst. Then, when I'd just started 6th grade, my religion teacher—who was about 18 and wore the hijab—gave this amazingly inspirational speech about it. She said that the hijab would allow people to see our iman (faith), and this would please God. I hung on to her every word.

Coming home that day, I realized how comfortable I felt wearing the hijab. I felt more connected to God, more pure and religious, with it on. I wanted to get even closer to God, so I decided to wear the hijab all the time.

Before I started wearing the hijab to school, I was treated like everyone else. I'd made a few friends in my 6th grade class. Although we didn't hang out outside of school, we were always talking in class about homework or giggling about silly things, like what the lunch ladies put in our food. And the other kids in my class were generally nice, too.

That all changed when I walked into class wearing the hijab. I felt so self-conscious, as if all eyes were on me. I was expecting my friends to come over to me, asking why I was wearing it. Yet they said nothing They just gave me these shocked faces, as if they couldn't believe it was me, Maria. I felt betrayed, angry, and sad. I wanted to explain to them why I was wearing the hijab, but they didn't even talk to me.

Lunchtime was much better. I always sat with a group of close friends from another class. Unlike the kids in my class, this group was ethnically mixed. My lunch friends were curious about my hijab but not turned off by it. It made me feel good that they cared enough to ask me about it, and they thought it was cool that I wanted to take my faith to the next level. I wished we were in the same class.

In the days that followed, I noticed my classmates acting like I didn't exist. I felt like some sort of an alien, a being that was totally different from everyone else, including my so-called friends.

They made no move to talk to me, which made me afraid to talk to them. I didn't want to risk being made fun of. One of them was one of the most popular girls in school, and I'd seen her and her friends from other classes cruelly tease other girls in public. Feeling like I didn't belong really hurt because I wasn't used to being isolated. But I knew I could turn to God.

After I began wearing the hijab, I started doing the five daily prayers. Kneeling down in prostration, I felt God was truly listening. When I prayed, total peace filled my soul. I confided in God, accepted him as my friend. I felt as if each and every thing I did and said counted and was important enough to be recognized. After praying, I knew that wearing the hijab was right for me and my relationship with God.

When they weren't ignoring me completely, my classmates whispered about me or gave me strange looks.

But in class it was hard to stay focused on my reasons for wearing the hijab. When they weren't ignoring me completely, my classmates whispered about me or gave me strange looks. Sometimes I was tempted to take off the hijab and show everyone that I had hair, too. I could look and be like them if I wanted.

The weeks wore on without a change. Once, when I felt like giving up, I called my cousin Uzma. I was hoping she would tell me it was OK to stop wearing the hijab. She didn't.

"Well, we told you it wasn't going to be easy," she said. "But now that you wear the hijab, you have to stick to it. I can only tell you to be strong and to not give up." I hung up feeling more hopeless and lonely than ever.

But right then I knew that even if she had told me to take off the hijab, I wouldn't have been able to. I realized that I wanted to test myself and my faith, to prove to myself how strong I could be.

I'd been crying and praying alone at home for about a month when my mom changed her attitude towards me and the hijab.

She said she could see what I was going through, my pain and determination, and she admired it. By accepting my decision, she gave me so much comfort and support. When I wasn't able to hold myself up after a hard day at school, she would hold me, saying soothing and encouraging words.

A few months after I started wearing the hijab, I arranged to pray Zuhr, the second daily prayer, in the assistant principal's office at lunchtime. (Two 8th grade girls I knew from duhrst told me she let them pray there.)

I'd spend the morning as the outcast in my class, but when the bell rang, I'd grab my prayer rug and leave it all behind. Praying helped me meditate on my inner self and relieve the stress from school. It made me feel as if it were only me and God in the same room, old buddies catching up on the day, on life.

When I finished with my prayer, almost half the period would be over. I'd head to the lunchroom and to my friends from another class. We'd chat about regular stuff, like what was going on in the news, and who got what on the math test. They accepted me as I was, and I felt like the true me. Then I'd go back to the classroom, back to being ignored.

Yet as time passed, I felt stronger and stronger about my faith, and I stopped feeling hurt when my classmates behaved like I didn't exist. With my mom's and God's help, I became completely confident about my decision to wear the hijab. Wearing it brought me closer to God, much closer than I ever imagined. By the last year of middle school, I didn't give my classmates' stares a second thought.

When I was in 8th grade my cousin Salma, who was 22, started calling me about once a month. She was exploring Islam, and she'd consult with me about our religion and how it fit into her life and what she was feeling. She wanted my advice, and it made me feel important.

So that summer, when Mom told me, "Guess what! Salma's started to wear the hijab too!" I felt pure joy and pride. I'd gone from feeling like a miserable outcast to a strong role model, surpassing even my own expectations.

Now, almost seven years after I first wore the hijab, I feel totally comfortable with myself. I've made friends in high school—both Muslims and non-Muslims—who respect me for who I am. I'm proud of my religion. I believe in my faith and I believe in my relationship with God.

Maria was 17 when she wrote this story.
She later attended Simmons College

YC Art Dept.

Why the Hijab?

By Maria Zaman

I'm a Muslim woman who wears the hijab, a headscarf that covers my hair, neck. and shoulders. Non-Muslims often ask me questions about it, usually the same things over and over. I wrote this series of questions and answers for everyone who doesn't know about the hijab. I might even start carrying it with me to refer to whenever I get tongue-tied.

Q: Do you sleep with that on?

A: No, I can take it off at home because the hijab is only to conceal my hair from men outside my family. I can show my hair to my father, grandfather, uncles, and brothers. I definitely don't keep it on all the time.

Q: Why do you wear it? I mean, you must be boiling in all this humidity.

A: Actually, I'm not too hot at all. I feel cool because I'm sheltering myself from the sun.

But that's not why I wear the hijab. It's a shield that hides my physical beauty. If I showed my hair, wouldn't I look more attractive? The hijab is a warning sign for men, saying, "Look out, 'cause I'm not available!"

I feel pious when I wear the hijab, as if I'm hiding something special. It's my way of presenting myself as a modest, respectable woman. I feel that I respect my body enough that I don't need to show it for others' pleasure. I feel I'm not a slave to the media's image of the perfect woman.

As a friend of mine once said, "The hijab forces people to see us for who we are on the inside. They have to judge us by our intelligence, not by how tight or short our clothes are."

Q: Why don't I see Muslim men covering themselves up?

A: It's mandatory for Muslim men to cover up from their navels to their knees. They are expected to dress decently in loose-fitting clothes, and to present themselves in a dignified and respectable manner.

Q: But why do Muslim women cover their hair, neck and shoulders when men don't have to?

A: Women have to cover more of themselves than men because Muslims believe God has given women more attractive features than he has given men. We also believe that women are less tempted by physical beauty than men are, so men don't have to cover themselves as much.

Q: How do you feel about wearing the hijab after September 11?

A: Ever since September 11 and the war in Iraq, it's become even more important for me to wear the hijab. I want to show Americans that Muslims are not those terrorists or extremists shown in the media, that real Muslims are caring, respectable, intelligent people.

Maria was 17 when she wrote this story.

Karolina Zaniesienko

I'm American First

By Zeba A. Khann

I am proud and content being an American. I refuse to be part of another culture. It's not that I don't have one. In fact, I have several: my ancestors came from the Middle East, Canada, parts of Europe, and Asia.

I would gladly be part of any one of these cultures if I lived in another country. But I don't. Whatever is considered the "American way" is really the only culture I want to be a part of.

There's nothing wrong with being from another country; in fact, America's diversity is what makes it so great. By becoming American, you don't stop being African or Asian or Italian. But there needs to be a stronger American spirit, and your first loyalty should be to the place where you live—the United States.

Many people, even those who have lived here for years, don't feel this way. Their first loyalty is to their own ethnic group or native country. Some of them refuse to learn the English language. Why? Where's their pride in being an American if they don't even speak English?

You can speak 20 languages if you want to, but if you live in the U.S., English should be one of them. If I were to move to France, I would learn to speak French because I would want to be able to communicate and get along in French society. I wouldn't expect the French to learn English just to accommodate me.

By not learning English, people hold America back—and they hold themselves back, too. They prevent themselves from enjoying many of the opportunities that are available to them. There are a lot of good jobs that you cannot get unless you speak English. And that job can mean more money and a better way of life.

By not speaking the language, people deprive themselves not only of economic opportunities, but political, educational, and social opportunities as well. How can we make friends with people from different ethnic backgrounds if we all speak different languages? How can we learn about each other's cultures? It's no secret that a lot of problems are created by a lack of communication. If we were able to communicate with the people around us, it would make us less suspicious of each other. It might even end much of the existing discrimination.

We have to be able to throw on our blue jeans and say in fluent English, "Yes, I am American."

In order to make life better for all of us, we have to be able to throw on our blue jeans and say in fluent English, "Yes, I am American." We have to dress more American, eat American foods, and take part in American celebrations. If you don't like hot dogs and football games, at least be willing to share in the spirit of Thanksgiving and the Fourth of July.

But that isn't all there is to it. The so-called American culture is more than blue jeans, hot dogs, and apple pie. It's a feeling that lets us know that no matter how different we are, we have at least two common bonds: our pride in being American, and our ability to communicate with each other effectively. If we all get together, maybe we can make America its own culture. The possibilities are endless.

Zeba was 18 when she wrote this story. She went on to attend Hofstra University and graduated with a degree in Interdisciplinary Studies.

Looking Over My Shoulder

By Abanty Farzana

Tuesday, September 11, 2001, seemed like any other day at my high school until I sat down in my 4th period government class, at around 9:15 a.m.

"Did you hear what happened?" asked my teacher. He was distraught, completely opposite from his usual outgoing, happy attitude. "Two planes just crashed into the World Trade Center," he said.

Shock. That's the only word to express how I felt. I just sat there in disbelief. Suddenly one of my classmates walked in and announced, "Another plane crashed into the Pentagon. And the World Trade Center just collapsed." Like a stampede, all the people in the class jumped up from their desks and ran to the windows, crowding around to see what used to be our view of the Twin Towers.

Those towers were the only part of the Manhattan skyline we could see from our Brooklyn school, because even the tallest buildings in our own borough couldn't block them. But that morning, the only thing we saw and smelled was black smoke across the sky. During the next period, the smoke became so strong that the fire drill lights started blinking.

I got out of school around 11 a.m. because of my internship, but I hurried home instead. I looked around the house for my father, but he wasn't there. I was worried. My father works in Lower Manhattan, not too far from the World Trade Center. But because he works at night and rarely in the morning, I tried to reassure myself that he must be fine. I just wished I wasn't alone in the house.

I found myself not only being afraid of another terrorist attack, but for my family's and my own safety.

I called my mother to tell her that I was fine, only to find out that my uncle, Mohammad Islam, actually worked in one of the towers. Just before my heart started pounding, my mother spoke two words that I'll forever be grateful for: "He's fine." It was such a huge relief.

My father came home 15 minutes later, and soon we were bombarded with phone calls from relatives in California, Texas, and other states, asking if we were all right.

Over the next couple of days, I felt like I was on an emotional roller coaster. Shock and disbelief gave way to numbness, which soon turned into sadness. But the most powerful thing I felt, which only developed the next day, was anger. I was furious at whoever was insane enough to take so many innocent lives and ruin so many others.

I soon learned the hijackers were believed to be Muslims. I didn't give them any sympathy for that, even though I'm Muslim myself. I think the terrorists learned some other book instead of the Islamic holy book, the Qur'an. Nowhere does the Qur'an condone terrorism or killing people. The hijackers' actions were disrespectful to Allah and to millions of Muslims around the world, who were suddenly associated with these insane attackers.

In fact, the hijackers put Muslims everywhere on the defensive. Soon I found myself not only being afraid of another terrorist attack, but for my family's and my own safety in my neighborhood and school. The next day, I heard on the news about attacks in America against Arabs and Muslims.

It scared me to death, thinking that I'd have to go back to school the next day in a building where some might hate me and "my people." I worried we might have a Columbine-style shooting at my school and that I or other Muslim students would be targets.

But I wanted to be strong for my 10-year-old brother, who had so much fear in his eyes. "Are there people in my school who hate Muslims too?" he asked. My parents and I just told him not to be scared and that nothing would happen to him.

Our fear was not irrational, though. The day we went back to school, my government teacher told the class that a student in another class had said, "We should kill them all," when asked about his feelings towards Muslims. That made me feel completely unsafe.

My father tried to reassure me after school that I'd be fine since I don't wear a hijab (a head covering) and the traditional clothing. It didn't make me feel any better. I was still scared, because I knew people didn't need to care what I wore to dislike me. The color of my skin and the way I look would be enough for them to decide how they felt.

When school resumed after the attack, my brother's classmates asked him where he's from and what religion he believes in. It bothered him. He felt that they were implying that he was one of the "bad guys," and it upset me that my brother had to deal with this. Even though he's young, he's not so young that he doesn't understand things.

In some of my classes that week, students lashed out against

Arabs and Muslims after seeing the footage of Palestinians rejoicing over the attacks. I overheard some classmates saying they believed that all Muslims were happy about it, that they'd do it again and that no one could be protected from them. They concluded that all Muslims believe in terrorism.

I don't think these classmates knew that I'm Muslim. Their comments bothered me, but I didn't want to have a confrontation in the middle of class, so I didn't speak up. Even when things are normal, I'm pretty quiet in class. I didn't want to start out the year being defensive when it was only the second week of school and I didn't know many people in my class.

Also, it was only a few people who had negative things to say, so I didn't let them bother me too much. I believe that most people know better than to judge a whole group by a few people's actions.

But some ignorant people are violent. By this time, I'd read about people who shot worshippers in a Texas mosque and a firebomb that was thrown at an Arab-American community center in Chicago. At school, I kept hearing about attacks against students in other schools. Someone said that Arab students at another Brooklyn high school were beaten up with baseball bats. My teacher had heard about two teachers in Connecticut who beat their Arab students. I didn't know whether any of these stories were true, but they still frightened me.

They watched as I took a book from my bag. I felt like saying, "I'm not gonna take out a bomb, OK?"

I also heard stories about Arabs assaulted while walking in their neighborhoods. I began to worry about my parents. Both worked very late and came home by themselves. "What if something happens to them on their way home?" I thought.

When I learned of threatening phone calls that my 16-year-old cousin Sabrina got, it only escalated my fear. She doesn't live far from my neighborhood, and the caller had cursed at her and her mother and told them to leave the country.

I figured the caller must've looked in the phone book, found the Arabic-sounding names, and then called and harassed the people listed. That possibility unnerved me because the phone book also gives the address of residents. I worried that ignorant people might show up on my front step.

Sabrina and our cousin Orin, who's 14, both go to my high school. They were just as frightened as I was, if not more. Their parents didn't want to leave them home alone anymore, and to my surprise, they didn't want to be alone either. They'd always enjoyed their independence before and liked having time alone.

"I heard about young girls getting abused and that scares me," said Orin. "I'd rather be around adults and surrounded by people. Now my parents either take me with them when they go out or leave me at my cousin's house."

My older cousin, in Boston, said that things had changed for her too. She was the only non-black person of color at her office, and it had never bothered her before. But in the days after September 11, she felt like she stood out. People stared at her when she walked down the street.

I know what she means. Weeks after the Twin Towers came down, I was still feeling uncomfortable in public. People on the subway or the bus never seemed to notice me before September 11. Afterwards, I felt like I turned their heads. They watched me when I took out a book from my bag. I felt like saying, "People, I'm not gonna take out a bomb, OK? There are insane people out there. I'm not one of them. I'm just as worried and nervous about another attack as you are!"

Some of my fears were realized when my uncle was attacked less than a month after 9/11. He was outside the store where he works in Brooklyn when two guys came by asking if he had money. He said no and they started pounding his head. They didn't have any weapons, but they were wearing big, sharp rings that cut his forehead and the back of his head.

After seeing him, his manager called the police. Paramedics came and bandaged his head. His face swelled up, and he suffered pain and bleeding for days after.

The police said that it wasn't a bias attack, but I find that hard to believe. Why would someone single him out at 2:30 p.m. on a busy street where so many different people were shopping? If the perpetrators wanted money, people carrying shopping bags would've been better targets. Why pick a South Asian man who's right in front of his workplace?

Now I think I'm angrier than I am afraid. It's frustrating to be grieving for so many lost lives and to be looking over my shoulder at the same time. My friends, family, and I lit candles at home on the Friday after the attack to remember those who lost their lives. I participated in the candle memorial because I love America. Even though I was born in Bangladesh, this is where I've grown up for the last 10 years. This is where my brother was born. This is where I have my memories of happy times and sad.

For a while after September 11, I felt that Americans were united against Muslims, but my opinion changed somewhat after seeing Islamic leaders help conduct memorial services at the National Cathedral and Yankee Stadium. There are plenty of Americans who can understand that this tragedy has upset Muslims too, and that we're not the enemy. While there are people who still look suspiciously at people of Middle Eastern or South Asian descent, I have to try not to let every one of them get to me. I have hope that the bias attacks will eventually stop, and that one day I won't have to fear for my family and myself.

Abanty was 16 when she wrote this story. She went on to attend Temple University, where she majored in journalism.

John Gaston

Walking While Arab

By Sara Said

Some names have been changed.

As a devout Muslim, I wear a scarf that covers my hair and neck. After the September 11 attacks, I became an object of attention.

Walking to school in New York City about a week and a half after the attacks, a man in his 30s or 40s riding his bike saw me and yelled, "I will kill all Arabs and I will show you!"

He yelled so hard I thought my eardrums would break. I felt like bursting into tears and running home. If he hadn't kept riding past, I would've been running like crazy.

But when strangers heard and saw the man screaming those terrifying words, they asked me, "Are you OK?" or said, "Just ignore him." Some smiled and tried to make me feel safe, which helped a little.

I felt relieved that they didn't act against me, and happy and thankful that they understood how I felt at that moment. I couldn't look up at their faces because I was trying to keep myself from crying. Still, I really appreciated their kindness.

At school that day, I felt that my mind was somewhere else. The man's screaming kept bothering me when I was in class. I was shaken, but I wasn't shocked by his hateful message. From the time September 11 happened, it was hard to avoid feeling hated because I am a Muslim.

Then and in the months that followed, many Muslims and Arabs all over the United States were discriminated against and attacked. Some were kicked off airplanes because other passengers didn't like the way they looked or dressed. At least six people were even murdered because their killers wanted to strike back at a Muslim or an Arab. Hundreds of other violent incidents were reported.

In school, I heard about people in New York City who were attacked both physically and verbally while going to their mosques, or who had their stores or cars attacked and damaged. And many, like me, were verbally harassed.

A man riding his bike saw me and yelled, "I will kill all Arabs and I will show you!"

After that man's threats and the looks that people gave me after the tragedy, I wanted to go back to my home country, Yemen, where people accepted me as a Muslim and an Arab. I didn't want to be in a place where people saw me as a terrorist. I didn't want to live someplace where every day I walked in the streets feeling like an alien in fear of being attacked.

I was afraid to go to school and leave the house wearing my veil. All my friends who wear veils had a hard time deciding whether we should continue wearing our veils in the streets, or keep them off until we got to school. On our first day back to school after the attacks, I decided to wear my veil—but I made my brother come with me. And in case my father couldn't pick me up at the end of the day, I kept jeans and a hat in my backpack to change into so people wouldn't realize that I'm a Muslim.

When we weren't in school, my Muslim friends and I locked ourselves in our homes, and the Arabs and Muslims that I knew in my neighborhood deserted the streets. But after a few days, my friends and I came to the conclusion that we were wrong to fear anyone but God. That helped us conquer our fears. However, our parents were strict about the time we came home. We had to be home exactly at 4 or they'd be ready to call the cops, because they'd worry something had happened to us. It was like living in a 24-hour fear movie.

After I got screamed at, I decided to tell my mom what had happened. But I didn't come right out and say it; first, I told her like it was a joke.

"You know what, Mom? Today, right, I heard this as a joke, right," I said. "There was this man who screamed at a Muslim and told her—ha ha—that he would kill all Arabs. Isn't that stupid?" Telling her that way helped me keep myself from crying. Then I said, in a low voice, "To tell you the truth, it happened to me."

My mom looked at me as if she wanted to know if I was for real. When she saw that I was, she prayed for our safety. "Ahmudi Rabic ineik ahsan min kahric," she said, meaning, "Be thankful to God you are in a better position than others." She meant I should be thankful that I wasn't physically hurt like others have been. My mom said to have faith in God, for he is the Protector.

My friends who wear the veil were also harassed around the same time. Lamya, 19, said two people gave her the finger, including a woman in a car who opened the car door to gesture at her. "I felt really bad when they did that," Lamya said, but it didn't surprise her.

Similarly, Khadija, 18, went out with her friends in the first week after the tragedy and saw three teenage guys. One said, "Oh, check this out, a terrorist is living in this neighborhood too."

"It hurt me," Khadija said. She also felt that she'd been harassed in school. On her locker, she'd had a sticker that said, "I love Allah." One day, she walked out of science class and saw that her sticker was torn and thrown on the floor.

"I went to my teacher, and before I'd finished telling her what happened, I was crying and screaming, 'Why did they do it?' I was so disheartened," Khadija said.

In one of her classes, a discussion on a poem about the World Trade Center led to religion. Khadija's teacher mentioned that she'd been to Arab countries. One of the students said, "Oh, my God, how could you go to such countries?" The teacher ignored him. Then another student said something like, "Oh yeah, Muslims believe in killing, and their religion teaches them that." Khadija was angry, but she didn't say anything. The teacher just gave the student a disapproving look.

When you know about people's cultures and religions, you don't depend on stereotypes to form your opinion.

Later, Khadija found a way to respond. Along with the president of the Bengali Society at our high school and me, she organized a meeting where we talked about what Islam really is. We explained that Islam in Arabic means peace and submission to God. Islam is based on the teachings of God as revealed to his last prophet, Mohammad, and teaches only peace, justice, and righteousness.

We organized the conference because we believe that education is the enemy of discrimination. When you know about other people's cultures and religions, you don't depend on stereotypes, which are often negative, to form your opinion of that particular group.

Teachers and students who came to the meeting said they were glad we'd organized it. It helped them understand what we were going through, and why we felt the media was playing a big role in creating hatred against us by focusing so much on

Arabs and Muslims who are terrorists.

These days, people still stare at me on the street, but not as much, and I'm no longer feeling scared. The fear that was caught in my heart has faded because I learned I must never allow fear to rule my life or conquer my dreams.

I keep in mind the nice people who supported me, helped me think more positively, and made me believe that there is more good in the world than there is bad. I will not let some people's ignorant hate become an obstacle and a barrier to living my life the way I want—as a Muslim, in the U.S.

Sara was 15 when she wrote this story. She later graduated from Brooklyn College with a degree in secondary education and history.

Kenneth Ng

Singled Out

By Sabah Kaid Aljahmee

"Fear and insecurity are the biggest challenges that I have to face because of my immigrant status," said Ibrahim (not his real name).

Ibrahim came to the United States from Yemen at age 12 with his family. He overstayed his visa and didn't get a green card to live in America legally. After September 11, Ibrahim started to wonder how long he'd be able to stay here, because of a U.S. government policy requiring immigrants from certain countries to register with immigration offices.

In 2002, then-Attorney General John Ashcroft announced the creation of the National Security Entry-Exit Registration System, or "Special Registration." Special Registration was put in place after 9/11 "to keep track of those entering and leaving our country in order to safeguard U.S. citizens and America's borders," according to the website of U.S. Immigration and Customs Enforcement (ICE). It requires visitors to the U.S. to register with ICE and update immigration authorities on their address and activities while they remain in the country.

But Special Registration doesn't apply to everyone. For one thing, it does not apply to visitors who don't need a visa to enter the United States for up to 90 days—in other words, visitors from the 35 countries included in our Visa Waiver Program—unless they have overstayed the 90 days. (Almost all these 35 countries are European, along with a few other wealthy nations like Japan.)

Special Registration also imposes special requirements on male citizens of Iran, Iraq, Libya, Sudan, and Syria, nations considered most likely to harbor terrorists. And during 2003, male visitors from a total of 25 countries who were already in the U.S. were required to register at ICE offices. Most of the 25 countries have a majority Muslim population, including Pakistan, Bangladesh, Indonesia, and Saudi Arabia.

Yemen was one of the 25 countries on the list, so Ibrahim, 18, went to immigration offices at the beginning of January in 2003. Once there, he felt weird and scared because he didn't know what was going to happen to him.

"They asked me personal questions, like how long I have been in this country. With who? Why?" he said. Then they took his passport and told him that they'd send him papers giving the date on which he should return to their offices.

"I wonder if I'll have to wear a sign that says, 'I am a Muslim and Arab,'" he said.

Ibrahim said he knew other members of the Muslim community who are waiting to hear what the government's decision will be. "They are scared about what's going to happen next and how they are going to support their families," he said.

Ibrahim feels Special Registration is ineffective as well as unfair, since it singles out law-abiding Muslims and real terrorists will not voluntarily show up at immigration offices. "I wonder if I stay any longer, if I'll have to wear a sign on me that says, 'I am a Muslim and Arab,'" he said.

Even Muslim immigrants with proper documentation have experienced fear about living in the U.S. since 9/11.

"Sometimes, I feel insecure because I am Arab," said Nasser Almasri, 18, who came here from Yemen when he was 16. "But I feel more comfortable than Arabs with no papers." Although none of Nasser's family had to go to immigration offices because they either have green cards or are citizens, he thinks that the registration law is unjust.

"The new registration law makes many difficulties for the immigrants who came here to have a better life, to support their families, and gain more education," said Nasser. He fears that government action could soon be taken against immigrants who are here legally. "I am afraid that Arabs and Muslims with papers could be kicked out from this country any minute," said Nasser. "Since 9/11, Arabs and Muslims with papers and with no papers are the same in Americans' eyes."

As a result, Nasser feels that his life in the U.S. has changed. Before 9/11, he considered America his second country. But after 9/11 and since the registration appeared, Nasser, who teaches 5th graders in an after-school program, feels like he can't think about his future career and dreams, which I can understand.

I'm originally from Yemen as well. Although I am here legally, I fear that I won't be able to fulfill my dream of becoming a pharmacist because there's no telling what new policies may arise that could single out Muslims even more.

"I know some people who have papers, but they left this country since the registration law appeared," Nasser said. Rather than getting kicked out by the government, "they said they wanted to leave this country by themselves, with their dignity."

Sabah was 18 when she wrote this story.

Getting My Green Card

By Fekri Kram

I arrived in the United States in 1999, when I was 9 years old. I didn't have a green card. A green card is basically a document saying that you have permission from the government to live long-term in the U.S. even though you're not a citizen.

I didn't have any choice about coming to the U.S. I was born in Tunisia, in North Africa. I lived with my mother, who was very poor, and two brothers and a sister. We lived in a pretty desperate situation and often didn't have enough to eat. When I was 5, a French woman bought me for $100 and eventually brought me to the U.S.

During the four years that I lived with her, she was so abusive that she nearly killed me. A month after we got to the U.S. I escaped from her and went into foster care. I had no way to contact my family back in Tunisia. I had no one.

I ended up in a residential treatment center (RTC). Besides dealing with the trauma from my past, I also had to endure teasing from the other kids in the RTC. I was Muslim, and I didn't speak English—only Arabic and some French. I dressed differently and prayed five times a day. Especially after 9/11, many of the others teased me and called me "terrorist." But I was just a kid who wanted to fit in and have friends, and their teasing made me feel as if I did not belong.

Once the staff took nine of us kids on a trip to Six Flags theme park. We were bumping along in the van, listening to hip-hop on the radio. Then the Biggie Smalls song "Juicy" came on the radio. As soon as Biggie said "blow up like the World Trade...," the other kids all looked at me. One kid, Jamal, said, "Fekri did it, you f-ing Muslim. Why did you do this to us? Go fly away on your carpet!"

One kid said, "Fekri did it, you f-ing Muslim. Go fly away on your carpet!"

I'd been told by many staff that kids would say things to hurt new people they didn't know. It still hurt so bad. I took in those words and held them inside. That night I was depressed, questioning God's doing, wondering why he would let them tease me like that.

It didn't stop there. Many staff would not let me say my prayers, and even though it's not allowed for Muslims to eat pork, sometimes I would be forced to because that was the only thing served for dinner. I'd tell them I wasn't supposed to eat pork, and they'd just say, "What are you going to eat, then?" So as a kid, I figured I didn't have a choice.

I wanted so much to fit in that I decided to convert to Catholicism, which was easy enough since my RTC was run by the Catholic Church. After that, things got a little better, but the kids still said things like, "Get your green card, you immigrant."

I got tired of dealing with the harassment, and I thought if I could just get my green card, maybe the teasing would finally end. I wanted people to see me as more than an African Muslim and an illegal alien. I wanted to do something for myself that would make people describe me as a person with people skills, someone who has been through a lot and wants to help others and not be looked at as different. Getting my green card seemed like an important first step.

I decided to speak to Paul, my social worker, to see if he could help me get my green card so I would be a legal resident of the United States and eventually get U.S. citizenship.

Paul responded by telling me, "It's not important." He said he was busy trying to deal with other issues, like older residents who had been in the RTC for years and still needed things done. Paul never seemed to make time for me because he had so many other cases. I got the message he did not want to work on my case, which was the biggest and most complicated.

Even though I had my Tunisian passport, no one had a copy of my birth certificate. I had no Social Security number, and I didn't speak English well enough to explain how I'd come to be in the U.S. or to help them figure out how to get the documents I needed. I didn't even know how they could contact my biological family back in Tunisia.

So it was hard for me to get anywhere. By 16, I started to realize that there were other reasons to have a green card. I needed to be able to work, and to work I had to be a legal U.S. resident. I learned that I also faced being deported if I got in trouble with the law and didn't have a green card. That ran through my mind so much because if I was deported back to Tunisia, I wouldn't know where my family was or what to do. I would be completely lost.

Meanwhile, staff had started talking to me about the process of aging out—leaving foster care when I turned 21. I realized that I needed things to start happening fast with my green card, because once I aged out, the foster care system would no longer help me get it. I didn't have many plans for my future because Paul never seemed to want to work on my case. I lost faith in him and decided to get my documents and green card myself.

Some staff I really respected encouraged me to do it on my own. They told me where to find the phone numbers for the Tunisian Embassy and the U.S. Immigration office. My first step was to call the Tunisian Consulate here in New York. I said, "Hello, my name is Fekri and I would like to get information so that I can become a legal U.S citizen." One embassy staff cursed me out in Arabic and English: "You f-cking Americans and your stupid country," he said. He seemed enraged at the fact that I wanted to become a U.S. citizen.

It would have been easy to give up at that point, but I persisted. The second person I called was Mr. Salah, at the Tunisian Embassy in Washington, D.C. He was much nicer. He told me he could help me get it done and he sent me the green card application.

I felt so relieved, but I was also overwhelmed because the application was only in French and Arabic, and I don't read either. So I asked Claude, a security staff at my RTC who spoke French, to translate.

The application asked for my name, where I was born, how I entered the U.S., and what I planned on doing with the green card. It also let me know what I could and could not do once I had the card. For example, I wouldn't be allowed to use the green card as an ID, and I couldn't travel outside the country for more than 90 days at a time or I'd lose my card.

In the meantime I set up an appointment at the Social Security office to apply for a Social Security number. I woke at 7 a.m. to go with a staff to the office with my RTC campus ID and passport.

At the Social Security office, we had to sit in hard chairs and wait for three and a half hours until my number was called. The office was hot, there were ripped things on the wall, the bathroom was dirty, and people were sleeping on the seats. The staff would yell "Next!" over and over.

But all my efforts paid off when I finally received my green card at 18. It took two years, but finally it was done. Mr. Salah also helped me get in contact with my mother and the rest of my family. I asked, "Since you work for the Embassy of Tunisia, is it possible to help me find my family?" He said, "Give me two weeks."

Sure enough, Mr. Salah called me at the RTC one day and said, "Your mother would like to speak to you." I got on the phone and they transferred the call, all the way from Tunisia.

I wanted people to see me as more than an African Muslim and an illegal alien.

"Fekrrri," she said, with an r that rolled like a boulder on a hill. I said, "Omi," which means "Mom" in Arabic. I had not spoken to her in 14 years. It felt great knowing that my family still has concern about me. They all told me they loved me. I will always remember that day.

I now have a new social worker, and I'm seeking help from him and my caseworker to set up a trip to Africa to visit my family. The funny thing is, Paul continues to keep in contact and lets me know when he hears something new about my family, like how they continue to ask when I'm coming to see them. I would have liked more help from Paul when I was getting my green card. But I learned that some people only want to help when they realize that you are willing to help yourself.

And when one person isn't helpful, you can't just get discouraged. You have to look around and find other helpful people, and then keep a good relationship with them. Sometimes you have to man up and take responsibility for the things you need done. You have to be your own support.

Fekri was 19 when he wrote this story.

YC Art Dept.

Lamis Aqel and Sara Said

Land of Conflict

By Sara Said

Lamis Aqel is a Palestinian teen living in Brooklyn. Lamis, 16, only lived in Palestinian territory for less than a year. Even so, she has felt the effects of the disastrous war that's been going on between the Palestinians and Israelis for more than half a century.

Israel—or Palestine, as it's known in the Arab world—is a holy place for Islam, Christianity, and Judaism. In ancient times, both Jewish and Palestinian people lived there together. Almost 2,000 years ago, the Romans drove most Jews from the land, though some remained. About 1,400 years ago, when Islam began, a majority of the land's population became Muslim.

Around the turn of the 20th century, some Jews around the world formed a movement called Zionism and began settling in Palestine in growing numbers. Zionists, some of them persecuted in other countries, saw their return to Palestine as a Jewish rebirth. In 1947, after the Holocaust, the United Nations recommended establishing an Arab state and a Jewish state side by side. By then there were about 600,000 Jews and 1.2 million Arabs in the land.

Arab nations rejected the UN recommendation but the Jewish side accepted it, and in 1948 they declared an independent state called Israel.

Neighboring Arab states sent in troops, and war broke out. Israel won control of most of the land, though two areas called the West Bank and Gaza were claimed for Palestinian Arabs. Many Arabs fled their homes and wound up as refugees in the West Bank, Gaza, and neighboring Arab countries, where they and their descendants remain today.

One of Lamis's cousins was killed while he was buying bread for his mother.

Lamis's grandparents were born in Ramallah, a major Palestinian city, but left in 1948. The war between Israel and its Arab neighbors made it difficult for Lamis's grandparents to find steady work, so they left behind their homes and their children.

First her grandparents went to Kuwait. But Kuwait would not grant them citizenship. Many Arab countries have refused to give Palestinian refugees citizenship. They argue that it's not because they don't want the Palestinians, but that giving Palestinians citizenship would destroy their right to return to Israel and the Palestinian territories.

Either way, the result is that many Palestinians are forced to live in terrible conditions within Arab counties including Kuwait, Syria, and Lebanon. Often they live in refugee camps where it's difficult to find employment.

So Lamis's grandparents moved to Jordan, an Arab country bordering Israel, where many Palestinians live. Unlike other Arab countries, Jordan has granted many Palestinian refugees full citizenship. Palestinians in Jordan can work and live as regular citizens, and Lamis's grandparents were able to send money to their children in Ramallah.

Lamis's mother and father both grew up in Ramallah. Then in 1967, when her mother was 19 and her father was 29, they were forced to leave the country. That year, as Arab nations prepared to attack Israel, Israel struck first. In the Six Day War, Israel took control of the West Bank, where Ramallah is, from Jordan.

Lamis's parents lived in fear through the horror of war and the occupation of their land by Israel. "When they left their home, they had to [look down] at the ground when they walked in the street. If they looked up, they may have gotten shot," Lamis said.

Her parents told her that the Israeli soldiers would touch, push, and boss the Palestinians while they walked in the streets. These things are still happening now, Lamis said. The Israeli soldiers are like "big bullies with machine guns."

Because her parents was living in harsh conditions and in fear, they moved to Jordan, where Lamis grew up. Conditions there were not very good either. Jordan is not a rich country and there aren't many jobs. So after things improved slightly for Palestinians in the 1990s, Lamis and her family tried moving back to Ramallah. They considered staying there permanently, and remained for several months.

"I was so happy to get there. I felt that I had arrived in my country," said Lamis, who was 12 at the time. All her sisters and brothers, aunts, uncles, and cousins were there in Ramallah. "I felt like we were all one family, all together," she said.

Lamis often went to the Al Aqsa mosque in Jerusalem, one of Islam's holiest sites. "I was sitting on the stairs and saw all the Muslims praying together," she said. "I was so happy. I saw the imam calling for prayer and the birds all gathered on the ground. There was a silence while we all prayed and it was peaceful."

Lamis was also scared, though, because the Israelis and Palestinians never stopped fighting entirely. Every time she went to the mosque, she watched Israeli soldiers grasping their weapons as Palestinians prayed. During her time in Ramallah, a battle broke out at the mosque. After some Palestinians threw rocks at Israeli policemen, hundreds of Israeli riot police stormed the mosque and opened fire with metal and rubber bullets, and tear gas. Three Palestinians died and 50 were injured.

"I was angry and I'm still mad" about the killings, Lamis said. Two weeks later she and her family went back to Jordan. Then, last year, they moved to New York. Lamis doesn't consider herself American or Jordanian, though. "Jordan is not my country," she says. "I feel more towards Palestine because they have always been going through so much suffering."

Now she worries about her family members who still live in Ramallah. Violence between Israelis and Palestinians has been fierce, and a few months ago, the Israeli army invaded the city. One of Lamis's cousins was killed while he was buying bread for his mother.

Lamis's parents lived in fear through the horror of war and the occupation of their land.

Lamis's mother told her what had happened when she arrived home from school. It was shocking to her. Lamis said she felt like her eyes were popping out and there were no tears. After that day, she said, "I felt tired and angry," and she couldn't concentrate on her schoolwork. Her cousin Fadi and her mom moaned and cried about her cousin's murder.

Lamis hears from her family in the West Bank about homes falling on people because of the Israeli missiles targeting Palestinian homes and buildings. She told me it's hard for her to hear about them suffering and living in terrible conditions.

There is often no water to drink, no food to fill their stomachs, and no electricity. Water pipes have been destroyed and damaged by Israeli soldiers. And often, when the Red Crescent and the Red Cross come to rescue Palestinians, the Israeli army has interfered with their rescue efforts. (Israeli forces say that Palestinian terrorist groups have used ambulances to hide militants and bombs.)

After her cousin was killed, Lamis's family began talking seriously about going back home to be with their family and reunited with their people. "I want to go back, too, and keep the Palestinian generation alive," she said. She keeps telling her friends that she will go if God wills it.

The conflict makes Lamis angry that her people have to suffer so much to remain in their homeland. "It makes me want to go back and fight for my land, because all of my family in Palestine are suffering and being killed," she said. "I wish I was still there."

Sara was 15 when she wrote this story.

No Place to Call Home

By Mohammad Ali

All my life, my family has been searching for a home. We lived in Baghdad, Iraq, during the first Gulf War in 1991, with bombs falling around us. Then we had to sneak out of the country into Jordan, where my father was not allowed to work. Finally, we tried to find a home in Europe—but ended up almost being sent to our death.

My name is Mohammad Ali and I am not a boxer. I come from the Middle East and I am Kurdish.

The Kurds are an ethnic group that no longer has a country to call its own. There are more than 25 million Kurds, and we mostly live in the mountainous parts of Turkey, Iran, and Iraq. This area used to be called Kurdistan, but before World War I, we lost our land.

Ever since then we've been fighting to get it back. We have

our own culture, and we want to be able to live according to our customs. But the countries Kurds have lived in are racist, and they have not granted us equal rights. In Iraq, it was illegal to have a Kurdish school, or to teach your kids how to write and read Kurdish. Many Kurds were killed because they wouldn't renounce who they are.

Sometimes I feel ashamed when people ask, "Where are you from?" I just say I do not have a country.

When I was young, I went to the region we still call Kurdistan three times. You cannot imagine how beautiful the place was. The house my family rented had a small orchard with fruit trees, and a little stream ran around the house. I felt that I belonged to this place. But instead of living there, my family was always looking for a home. Sometimes I feel ashamed when people ask me, "Where are you from?" I just say to them that I do not have a country.

I was born in Kuwait and so were my parents, but there people speak Arabic and not my language, Kurdish. Once I asked my father, "Why are we in this country and not in our native country?" My father told me how my grandfather had moved from Kurdistan to Kuwait more than 40 years earlier because Kurdistan is very poor. In Kuwait, my family had a good life.

But in 1989 we moved to Iraq, where my father had some relatives. Iraq is north of Kuwait and south of Turkey. Like Kuwait, it is a country rich with oil. Baghdad was beautiful then. My house was big, and outside we had a garden scented with the beautiful fragrance of jasmine flowers. My parents' faces were so happy that, if you saw them, you would know they were thinking, "Wow, this will be our country." They dreamed we could make Iraq our home.

Our lives were good until Iraq started a war with Kuwait because Saddam Hussein, Iraq's leader, wanted their oil fields. To get their homeland back, Kuwait called for help from the U.S., and the Gulf War began in 1990. It didn't last long, but in Iraq, people suffered a lot from the bombs and from not having food, electricity, or medicine for a long time after the bombing stopped.

At the time of the war I was about 7 years old. The U.S. was bombing Iraq in the morning and in the night. The first attack was on the electricity building, and the power went out for the rest of the year. My house used to shake every time a bomb hit the ground, and when the house shook more, that meant that the bomb was closer to where I lived.

Everything was scary. I used to stay home all the time, sometimes inside the garage or the garden. It felt like jail. I used to sleep when the sun set and wake up at sunrise because we had no lights.

In those days, life felt like a dark sky. During the war most countries stopped trading with Iraq, so there was very little food or medicine in the country. People couldn't work, so they sold their cars and things from their houses. Still, they were starving.

After the war Iraq was powerless, and the Kurds started to take back much of their land in the north. Their land is the most beautiful part of Iraq—green and mountainous. Saddam Hussein knew that if the Kurds were to get back all of their land for good, he would lose much of Iraq. He began killing Kurds, whether they lived in the north or in Baghdad; eventually his government killed more than 15,000 Kurds.

I had felt that Iraq was my country, but my feelings changed when the people and the Iraqi government turned against the Kurds after the war. I felt that I was not Iraqi, but a Kurd.

My family escaped the killings, but Saddam Hussein also made a law to make all the Kurds leave Baghdad and go to the south and west of Iraq—to the desert. Those places were dangerous and very poor, so my father said we had to leave Iraq. At the time, the only place Iraqis could go was Jordan. It cost a lot to go, and we had to sneak out of Iraq to get there.

It was a long way to Jordan, more than a day's journey by bus along a highway surrounded by black rock. But once we got there, the first few months were like heaven. I had almost everything I wanted. I was always with my two cousins and my brother, going around the city.

To me this life was cool, but my parents did not feel the same way. They wanted to get out of Jordan because we were being discriminated against. My father wasn't allowed to work and I wasn't allowed to go to school, because we were considered only temporary refugees; after six months, Iraqi passport holders had to pay a little each day they remained in Jordan. Besides this, the police were racist and would mistreat those who weren't Jordanian citizens. Sometimes they would send them back to their home countries.

I was afraid Jordan would be the final chapter of my life's book, and the end would be in Iraq.

My father wanted to go to Europe, where he had friends who seemed to have good lives. So he got us fake visas and we didn't tell anyone that we were leaving until the last minute. We got on the plane without problems, and I felt like I was on top of the world. I was wishing for a new life where everything would be perfect.

But when we landed in Hungary and went through customs, the officials found out the visas were fake. My legs were heavy; I couldn't stand. I hoped it was just a dream and that they would wake me up before it became real.

They put us in a refugee camp and kept us there for 21 days. It was like a jail: eating your lunch, then going back to your room or watching the TV. After three weeks, the Hungarian authorities made us leave the country. We flew to Egypt, then to Greece, looking for a place where we would be allowed to stay. Finally we were sent back to Jordan. We had heard that people like us who were sent back there had been killed. I was so scared getting off the plane in Jordan; I was afraid this would be the final chapter of my life's book, and the end would be in Iraq.

My father asked the Jordanian airport officials to call the United Nations to help us. At first, they told us a car was coming to take us to Iraq, and we were all thinking how we would kill ourselves before we'd let that happen. But a while later, a man came from the UN to talk to us. We told him everything we'd been through, and when he made calls to investigate our story, he found that it was true.

We were told the UN would grant us refugee status, but first we had to wait. So we stayed for about three weeks in the Jordan airport. The men slept in a waiting room, and my mother, sister, and youngest brother slept in a small room in a woman's bathroom. After that, the UN began giving us money so we could stay in Jordan temporarily, and I was allowed to go to school. I was happy because I'd been out of school for almost two years.

A few weeks after I finished the year, my family was granted entry to the United States. We were so excited. Everybody in Jordan said to us, "You will have the best life."

People in the Middle East were always talking about America. They said that when you come here, the government gives you a house and money every month. They said you don't have to work, only go to school and have a lot of time with your relatives. I believed them. I was excited to move here and make America my home.

When we first got to New York, my aunt—who had been living here for six or seven years—told us how hard our lives would be. For the first few days we stayed with her. She had a nice apartment, a car, and enough money to send to her family back home, but like most immigrants, she'd had to earn everything she had.

During those first few days, I went to Manhattan and admired the reflection of the sun on all the tall glass towers. Seeing all the beautiful houses and new cars in my aunt's neighborhood made me feel that it would only be a matter of time until I could have a good life like everyone else in America.

But when we moved into the apartment my aunt found for us, we were shocked. It was small, old, and full of mice and cockroaches. We slept without blankets and pillows, and furnished the house with things from the garbage: an old TV, a carpet, and some other furniture. It was a big shock for my family to be living in worse conditions than we knew in Jordan. My mom began saying she wanted to go back. My dad was quiet.

My aunt used to come every day and tell us this was only the beginning, and things would get better. Still, we felt lost. At least in Jordan we knew how to speak Arabic and used to get money from the UN. Here, we had no money. Yet we had relatives in Jordan who used to call us, expecting my parents to send money every week. My parents sent something when we had it, but most of the time we were too poor. Our relatives didn't believe that we didn't have money. They think that if you are in America, you are rich.

I feel that I'm losing what I learned about the Qur'an and the history of my people.

My father found work driving for a car service in Brooklyn. He used to come back at midnight so tired that he would only eat and then sleep until he had to go to work again. Sometimes I didn't see him all day. My mother didn't work because my younger brother was only 3, and also because in the Middle East, wives don't usually work. It was hard to get by, but we didn't want to give up our culture.

When school started, I was in 8th grade. My first week, I was scared. I thought, "How am I going to make them understand me?" I was like a statue in class. I knew only "yes," "no," and "English." When students or teachers asked me questions, I'd say, "No English."

Out of my whole class, only my sister and one other student, from Syria, could speak Arabic. I had no choice but to practice my English, and within a year, it had become my third language. I didn't speak it perfectly, but America became a better place once I could speak English. I made friends, and felt less like an outsider. I also learned about other people. I never knew that Christianity had divisions like Catholic and Protestant. And Latino people—I'd never heard of them. I was really surprised to find so many Americans speak Spanish.

But I didn't feel completely accepted. I found out that there are stereotypes about Muslims. Some people think that all Muslims are dangerous terrorists; we're not. Some of my friends used to ask me questions like, "Did you kill Jewish people? Did you bomb somebody?" I had to say, "No, no." Sometimes it made me mad, but I think people like to learn about other peoples and countries, so I'd just answer their questions honestly.

I also found there were things in American culture I didn't want to pick up, like the way kids in this country don't listen to their parents. It seems kids here have more power than adults, because parents and teachers aren't supposed to hit their kids. In the Middle East, parents hit their kids and if you have an attitude at school, teachers will hit you. I think that's why kids there are mostly good in school: They stop misbehaving after getting hit a lot. Here, when you do something wrong in school, they take you to the detention room and later you go back to class like you didn't do anything. I had friends who misbehaved just to get out of class.

Another thing that bothers me is that when a kid in the U.S. gets to 18, their parents don't always have a say in their lives anymore, and the kids usually leave their parents. In the Middle East, most kids live at home until they get married, and then they live either with the husband or wife's parents.

I don't want to give up those aspects of my culture. But immigrant kids who came when they were young seem much more eager to become American. Often, they don't know how to speak their parents' language, and they don't hold onto their home cultures. They say, "I'm American; that's it."

I feel glad to speak my own language at home, and read Arabic newspapers, watch Arabic TV, and listen to Kurdish music. But I hate that I no longer get lessons in the Muslim religion at school. I used to take a religion class every day growing up. Now, I feel that I'm losing what I learned about the Qur'an and about the history of my people, even though I study it at home.

And I don't pray five times each day like I used to. Every Muslim is supposed to pray five times a day from the age of 7 until the last day of his or her life. In the Middle East, we used to go to a prayer room at school. Here, I know I can't leave the classroom for 15 minutes each morning and afternoon.

My parents warn me to follow my own culture while taking advantage of the good things America offers, like a good education. They talk to me about wrong and right, but what they really want is for their kids to have a better life than the life they had. In Iraq my father was an architect, but his jobs here have been awful. He always says, "Do you want to work in a car service and be afraid all the time that you'll be killed, or do you want to be a doctor and help people?"

Still, my father wants to stay in America for the rest of his life because he is sure that this country is stable. Every year, the countries in the Middle East seem to get worse. I think the situation won't improve in those countries until we stop having dictators there, and begin using the same system as the United States—with institutions like the Supreme Court, Congress, and an elected president—so no one will have too much power.

I intend to go to college in America, but every day I think of moving back to the Middle East and staying for the rest of my life. I really want to live in the north of Iraq where there are Kurds. I hope in the future that I will have a country, but I know that Kurdistan won't be a country unless the United States were to force the Middle East to give land back to the Kurds. I don't think that will happen. So I think I will never have a land I can truly call my own.

Mohammad was 16 when he wrote this story.

YC Art Dept.

Not My Father's Daughter

By Sarvenaz Ezzati

In July I got a letter in an airmail envelope with Islamic stamps and Farsi writing on it. I immediately recognized that it was from Iran, the country I fled with my mother nine years ago, when I was 8. The sender was my father. Even though I haven't seen him in more than seven years, I'm still afraid of him.

I've always felt that if my father wanted to he could take me back to Iran. And since a girl belongs to her father like property there, he would have the right to marry me off to someone of his choice and get a dowry in exchange. Many times he threatened my mother that he would kidnap me and take me back to Iran. This caused me to be very wary of all Iranians, because I know how persuasive my father can be. If he said the right words, he could get anyone to help him.

When we first came to this country and socialized with other

Iranian families, adults would casually ask me questions about my mother and myself, and then convey the information back to my father. We soon learned to avoid other Iranians—especially Iranian men.

Then one day last summer, I heard two Iranian men on the train speaking Farsi, fluently and eloquently. I became very emotional and depressed. I realized how much of my Iranian culture and heritage I had given up because I was trying to protect myself from my father. I will probably never again dance the special Persian dances I once loved. Or attend festive parties like the ones I remember going to with my parents in Iran, where all generations celebrated together, guests were treated like royalty, and everyone shared huge plates of delicious meat stews and rice. For a moment, these happy memories allowed me to forget the dark side of thoughts about my father and my country.

Iran is now a place I fear and would never go back to voluntarily. It's a very religious and old-fashioned country. Women are supposed to be passive and quiet, and they are considered the weaker sex, mentally and physically. When the Ayatollah Khomeini seized power in 1979, overthrowing the Shah of Iran, he wanted to lead the country with the laws of the Qur'an, the Islamic holy book.

I realized how much of my Iranian heritage I had given up because I was trying to protect myself from my father.

Through his own personal translations of the Islamic laws, Khomeini took the rights of women away, forcing them again to wear black chadors (a veil that covers the entire body), denying them educational opportunities (the majority of Iranian women were illiterate), and telling Iranian men that knowledge for a woman was dangerous because women are not capable of working and making decisions for themselves.

The radical change from the Shah, who was very modern in his ideas about women's roles, to the repressive Ayatollah Khomeini literally happened overnight. One morning my mother woke up and realized she was the property of my father and that all her rights had been taken away. She also knew that any educational opportunities I would have had under the Shah were now nonexistent. We were like free birds suddenly trapped in a cage of religious oppression and darkness.

As the country became more oppressive, my mother's life there became unbearable. My mother speaks five different languages, was a straight-A student in high school, and upon graduation at the age of 18, began teaching Air Force pilots how to speak, read, and write English. But she never went to college because her father felt she should be married and that college for a girl was a waste of money.

When my mother married my father, she loved him and looked forward to a happily-ever-after relationship despite warning signals, like the other girlfriends he flaunted. It wasn't long after they were married that my father started to lie to my mother and sleep around. When he was angry, he beat her.

Here in the U.S., I've been raised to think of myself as equal to men and to make decisions for myself.

My father's approach to running his business was no better than his approach to marriage. Eventually, dishonest business dealings landed him in jail. Since my mother had helped out in his business, she knew the authorities were preparing to come after her, too. This hastened her decision to flee the country.

Here in the U.S., I've been raised to think of myself as equal to men and to make decisions for myself. I fear going back to Iran because I would not be able to go to college, have a career of my own, or even wear what clothing I like. I know that I could never live like the many Iranian women who take orders from their husbands and are financially and socially dependent. If a woman is not married in Iran, or if she is divorced, she is considered rotten, like spoiled milk. I could never survive in such an oppressive environment.

Young women in this country take for granted that they can go to college, dress how they please, and choose for themselves who they will marry. I, on the other hand, am always afraid that I will lose my opportunities to get an education and start my own career. I fear that I will end up married to a man like my father.

When I received my father's letter, my feelings of fear mixed with distrust. Because of the person he is, I know that even a letter that says nice things may contain danger.

My mother and I left Iran after struggling for four years to get green cards. My father promised to join us in the United States once he took care of his business. (Even after everything he did to her, my mother was willing to give him another chance.) But after three years he told my mother that he wanted us to return to Iran instead.

His reason was that he didn't want to give up his $1 million business in Iran. He told us that the situation for women in Iran had improved. But he was lying—Iranian women still had no rights. This didn't seem to bother him. He just didn't want to give up his business. I felt abandoned because his money meant more to him than I did.

I wasn't really surprised to get a letter from my father because occasionally he sends me something saying that he still thinks about me. He sometimes sends me gifts from Iran, telling me he cares for me, and that any unhappiness I feel is because of my mother. His gifts always feel like bribes to turn me against my mother. Instead, my trust in him lessens with every gift.

But there was something in this letter that I never expected. My father said that it was his duty as a father to pay for my college education—a bill my mother can't pay alone.

Now I feel that I'm being bribed once again, but the stakes are higher. He's willing to pay for my entire college education. This could be the chance of a lifetime. Since my grades are average, it's not very likely that I can get a full scholarship or grant. And it would be a big luxury if I could graduate college without a loan to pay back afterwards. With the money my mother would save, she could afford to send me abroad to study in London or Paris, and give me extra spending money.

Yet I feel like I'm being bought, and that if I accept the offer I would be letting my father off the hook. For the price of my college education, my father would want forgiveness and a second chance to be the father he never was.

I have to make my decision soon and it isn't an easy one, not like winning Lotto, where someone hands me a big fat check with no strings attached. After all, why would he make this offer without expecting me to allow him into my life again? If he pays, he could expect me to play the role of dutiful daughter. And, if I accept, I'll be committed to a relationship with him that I might not be ready for.

Sarvenaz was 17 when she wrote this story. She graduated from high school and college and became a school teacher.

University of Kitchen?

By Orubba Almansouri

"We're halfway through the summer. Are we going to New York or what?" I asked my older sister Yasmin. She had come to visit us at our house back in my country, Yemen. We were in the room we'd shared until she got married and moved away.

"Do you really want to go?" she replied, opening the Kit Kat bar she had in her hand.

"Yes and no," I answered as I lay down on my bed. "I want to stay here for you and all our extended family, but I also want to see Dad and New York City."

"What's the rush, then? It's not like you're going to school when you get there," she said.

In my family, most men believe that the best place for a woman is in the house and the best job for us women is to cook, clean, and raise a family. Many girls in my family—including

Yasmin—stop going to school before they reach high school, and none have gone to college. Girls live with their families until they are 15 or a little older, and then it's time to say goodbye to being single and hello to marriage.

My religion, Islam, is not against girls being educated. In fact our Prophet Mohammed, may peace be upon him, said that we should seek education even if we have to go to China for it. The problem isn't my culture either, since many Yemeni girls are educated and have jobs. Where my family's tradition came from, I don't know. But so far, no one has broken it.

After that, I saw my father as someone who really cares about his daughters' education.

I never imagined my destiny would be any different. In my country I was an excellent student and teachers loved me. In 7th grade, I was first in my class. They put my name in big letters on a piece of paper and hung it up in the main hallway. I felt so proud of myself.

I didn't mind leaving school at any time, though, because I knew the path girls in my family followed and I didn't expect anything else. When we came to the United States the first time (when I was 5—we stayed for a few years), my older sisters were teenagers and they didn't get a chance to go to school, even though they really wanted to go and learn English. So when I was 14 years old and I heard that we were moving back to the U.S., I figured I wouldn't be going to school anymore.

Then we got to New York, and my dad announced he was planning to enroll my sister Lebeya and me in school. I was surprised. From what I used to see on TV, American high schools were another planet compared to schools in Yemen. I wasn't used to going to school with boys, or talking to them. In fact, I was a little worried: I'd heard that many Yemeni students who go to American high schools start to do what the other kids are doing, like having relationships and even drinking, neither of which is allowed by my religion. I'd expected my dad would want to keep my sister and me away from this environment. (My mom wants us to be educated, as she never had the chance to be, but like most Yemeni women she follows her husband's decisions.)

But my dad was determined. When my oldest sisters didn't go to school in New York, that affected their lives and his. They couldn't go out alone because they didn't understand English and couldn't communicate. My dad had to translate for them at doctors' appointments. When we moved to New York, he said putting my sister and me in school would help us become independent so we could help ourselves when necessary.

For my part, I decided that since I had the chance to go to school, I would definitely take it. Today my sisters are both married and have children sweet as honey, but they still wish they had gone to school here and learned to speak English. I saw from my sisters' experience that education was the best thing for me, and I felt that going to school might be fun and a way to get out of the house. I had no idea what it would come to mean to me.

While we were getting records and report cards sent from Yemen to New York so my sister and I could enroll here, the men in my extended family started telling my dad that we would get ourselves into trouble and hurt the family's reputation. They thought that high school in America would Americanize us, causing us to drop the traditions we'd been learning our entire lives and pick up others.

One day my dad was on the phone with one of my cousins and I heard some of my dad's replies. (It's not my fault he thought that I was sleeping when I wasn't.) They went like this:

"They are my daughters and I have raised them right. I know what is good for them."

"It's none of your business."

"I don't care what they say, I have listened to you guys once and I won't make that mistake again."

After I heard that, I was saying to myself, "Way to go, Dad!" I saw my father as someone who is ready to make a change and someone who really cares about his daughters' education; I saw him in a way that made me feel proud to be the daughter of Ali Almansouri. I knew that my dad had put all his trust in us, and this made me want to be on my best behavior.

My first day at Brooklyn International High School was scary because I was starting 9th grade at the end of September and I was the new girl. I felt lonely at first, but luckily my English was OK from living here as a kid. By second period I'd talked to two Hispanic girls and we became friends. My teachers were so nice to me; they helped me when I needed help and they always asked me how I was doing. I began to love school once again. I worked hard and got excellent grades. My classmates started telling me, "You're so smart."

I don't believe that I'm as smart as they say, but I do believe that I am clever. Because I did well, ideas of actually graduating started coming into my head. My love for school grew, especially when I learned new things, went on trips, or met new friends.

"You know that I will be the first girl from our family to actually go to college," I said one day to my sisters and a group of other girls, while we were sitting together talking.

"Yeah, and you'll go to the University of Kitchen," my younger cousin said.

"And earn your cooking degree," my sister added.

Then they all started laughing, including me. "You'll see, when I become the first Almansouri girl to go to college and break the 'girls don't go to college' rule," I said. "You'll see what I will do."

The truth is, though, that there is always a question mark over my future. In spite of the things I overheard my dad say on the phone, his decisions about my future are not all made yet. My dad doesn't really follow up on my schoolwork, and when opportunities come up—like leadership programs or after school activities—it's not easily that he lets me participate.

I think that even though he put me in school, sometimes he still thinks the way other men in my family do. This worries me, because it makes me think he may not allow me to finish the path that he let me start. However, if I give him a great speech about why he should let me do some extracurricular thing, and if I'm persistent, he usually gives in. I think that when I put it in his head that I can benefit a lot from these things, he sees it, and that gives me hope for the future.

My being allowed to finish high school and go to college depends on two people: Dad and me. I will never disobey him because he is everything to me. My basic hope is that we don't go back to Yemen before I graduate from high school. Then, if my dad lets me, I'd prefer to put off marriage until I am settled in college.

What will actually happen, I don't know. My dad hasn't told me what he's thinking. Even though I hate not knowing what's going to be next, in another way I don't want the topic to come up yet. I'm afraid of the answer I'll get, in case it's a "no." Anyway, as they say, you have to walk up the ladder step by step or you'll fall down.

When I'm feeling hopeful, I think my dad will let me go to college. I want to attend a good college like Columbia University, major in English or journalism, and also study biology. I see my future as a finish line with red and white stripes, and I see myself crossing the line, then getting my prize—in other words, working in a career and feeling true power and independence. I also want to feel useful to the world and to people around me. I want to learn more and be an educated person.

Sometimes, though, I feel that everything I do is for no reason and that I will never be able to go to college or even finish high school. I worry that if I do graduate from high school, my dad will say, "I already let you finish high school and we don't have women who go to college in this family." I worry about the pressure that will be on him if he does let me go to college. Our family made such a big deal about us going to high school, I can't imagine what they would say about college.

When I hear things from my family like, "Girls your age are getting married and soon it will be your turn," those comments are like rockets landing in my ears. I find a place to be alone and think to myself, "All this hard work, these top grades, these compliments, for what? For me to remember when I'm seasoning the soup. Why did they put me in the race when I had no interest in participating? They put the idea in my head, made me like it and actually work toward something—all so that when I reach the finish line they'll tell me I can't cross it."

I imagine watching others cross the line without me, and put myself down for all the time I spent dreaming of things I want to accomplish. "Maybe it's not time, Orubba," I think. "Maybe the girl who will break your family's record hasn't been born yet."

I think to myself, "All this hard work, these top grades, for what? For me to remember when I'm seasoning the soup."

With that I cry myself to sleep. Sometimes I even have nightmares about not finishing high school. A lot of people think that it's no big deal; I'll get married and my husband will give me everything I need. But that's not enough for me because I want my life to have different flavors and taste them all, not just repeat the same flavor over and over every day. I also want to feel that I'm prepared if something happens to my husband. How will I feed my children? I want to have a weapon in my hand and education is one weapon that never hurts anyone, but actually helps.

In Yemen, I always thought that going to college was a good thing for girls, but I didn't feel envious of the girls from other families who could go. Since I came to the U.S., though, I have been thinking more about my future. I want more out of life. Because I see college as a possibility for me, but not a sure thing, today I feel envious toward Yemeni girls who know they can go to college.

Sometimes I get mad that my family keeps on pushing boys

to go to college, even though most of them don't have any interest, while some of us girls are ready to work for it and never get a chance. Other times, I tell myself that whatever education I end up with is better than nothing. I'm even a little afraid of going to college in case I fail. I'm torn between two things, but the tear is not straight down the middle. I'm happy that my obsession with success is greater than my worries.

Now I'm a junior, my grades are still excellent, and my desire to live my dream is greater than ever. I agree with some of my family's traditions, like girls not going out alone and not sleeping at anyone's house outside the family. But the education issue is too much. If they give all us girls a chance and support us, we can help our family reach higher than ever before. If I go to college, I'll open a path and be a role model for future generations of girls in the family, teaching them not to give up.

If my father's decision is for me to go to college, he will raise his head high and tell everyone who wanted to stand in my way that they were wrong; that he is happy and proud about giving us a chance that a lot of parents in my family took away from their girls. I want him to be really pleased with what I accomplish.

Everything I become will be because of the trust he gave me. I will keep my religion and my traditions, but I will follow my dreams as long as I know that what I'm doing is right. I have no problem with cooking and cleaning, as long as it is a side order with my dream. But if my dad doesn't support my dream, then everything that I have planned for won't be. That's what causes me nightmares instead of dreams.

Orubba was 16 when she wrote this story.

Forced to Marry Young

By Sadia Jahangir

All names have been changed.

My close friend Nadira and I met in our junior high school English class. We're both from Pakistan. I came here from Lahore, the second biggest city in Pakistan, when I was 12, and Nadira was 13 when she came from a village called Borewaal.

We both spoke the same language, Urdu, and liked to read novels in Urdu and watch Pakistani dramas on the PTV Prime channel. We'd go to each other's houses and sit together and talk for hours about school, movies, and our goals for the future. I want to be a doctor and Nadira wanted to be a lawyer. On weekends we'd go to the park and then sometimes to Pizza Hut.

Whenever I needed someone to share my happiness, or a shoulder to cry on, I always went to her. Even after we started going to different high schools we still called each other every day and hung out on weekends.

Then, when she was 17, Nadira suddenly went back to Pakistan to marry a man that her parents picked out for her. When she told me she was going to leave—only a few weeks before it was going to happen—I was flabbergasted and heartbroken.

We'd never really talked about marriage, although one time in junior high school Nadira told me that she suspected she'd get married at a young age. I didn't pay much attention to it and said, "Don't worry, it won't happen." Unfortunately, I was wrong: in the middle of her junior year, she came home from school one day and her mother said, "Your cousin got married. And we think it is time for you to get married, too."

I didn't have a problem with the fact that Nadira's parents had arranged her marriage—I am going to have an arranged marriage, too. That's traditional in Pakistani culture, and I think it's OK. I trust my parents to know who is bad and who is good, and to know what's right for me. They have raised me and they know what I like.

My parents will first let me study and stand up on my own feet—then marriage will come into my life.

But my parents will first let me study and stand up on my own feet—then marriage will come into my life. My father's dream is to see me as a doctor, so I think he'll try to find a guy who will accept me and my career. What bothered me about Nadira's situation was that her parents were making her get married so soon, and pulling her out of school to do so. I didn't think that was fair.

I was upset she was leaving school and probably ending her education. In traditional Pakistani culture—especially in villages like the one Nadira's family comes from—a girl who gets married is supposed to focus only on her new family, and not her education or career.

Nadira's parents had told her months earlier that they had

chosen the guy who would be her husband: her 22-year-old cousin, Ahmed. In Pakistani tradition, it is common for first cousins to marry each other, and Nadira was OK with the idea of getting married to Ahmed. They knew each other in Pakistan and she thought he was nice. He was very attached to her father and her father liked him.

But her parents hadn't said when she would marry him, so she was shocked when her mother gave her the news. I would have been shocked, too. When she told me, I wanted to know how she felt. Had she argued with her parents?

Nadira felt her parents were rushing her into marriage because they didn't trust her.

Nadira said she was depressed. "I've just started to live a teenage life, and now I have to take a wife's responsibility on my shoulders," she said. Still, she didn't express these feelings to her mother. "I was looking at her eyes that were filled with joy. I didn't want to ruin her happiness," she said.

She also thought that if she didn't do what her parents told her, she'd be harming their reputation, which is hers, too. From the time we're young, Pakistani girls are taught to think about our reputation. Before doing anything we have to ask ourselves, "Will it hurt my reputation?" Not going through with a marriage that's been arranged damages a Pakistani girl's reputation, along with her family's.

Besides this, Nadira was afraid of what her parents would do if she refused the marriage. Once they'd told her that if she didn't get married to a person they chose for her, then she couldn't stay in their house. So, Nadira said, "I didn't have the guts to reject it." She simply accepted her sudden marriage and told herself that's what was written in her destiny.

Many Americans might be surprised that Nadira didn't stand up to her parents, but I wasn't. Most Pakistani girls don't have the strength or desire to go against their parents. If you disobey them or talk back, it's considered rude and disrespectful. If you are disrespectful to your parents, then nobody in your family respects you. Plus, it's considered a sin in our religion, Islam, if you don't obey your parents.

I've never gone against my parents, because my love for them makes me want to listen to them and respect their wishes. But if my parents want me to do something, they first ask me my choice, and they don't force me into things. I consider myself lucky that my parents trust me. They often tell me, "We know that you won't let us down."

Nadira, on the other hand, felt her parents were rushing her into marriage because they didn't trust her. "They think I will blend into American ways" and not get married, she said. By American ways, she meant the way that girls here live with their boyfriends without being married. Her parents thought if she didn't get married soon, she'd have a boyfriend and have relations with him.

Nadira couldn't believe her parents thought this of her. "How can they think I'd stoop so low?" she said. "I never even talked to a boy in front of them."

In Pakistani culture, it is considered disrespectful if a teenage girl plays with a boy or hangs out with a male other than her father, brother, husband, or fiancé. My parents share this culture, but they let me stay late at school if I have to, and let me go out alone. I've promised them I won't do anything that will hurt their reputation, and they take me at my word. I follow their wishes and they listen to mine.

I felt angry about Nadira's situation. But when I talked to her two weeks after the initial news of her marriage, she told me she was feeling better about getting married.

"At first I wasn't happy because I thought this meant I'd never be able to go to college," said Nadira. But after she got engaged, Ahmed came to visit her. She felt comfortable talking to him, and he supported her wish to continue getting her education. Ahmed lives in Islamabad, a big city in Pakistan where there are colleges with good law programs. When she moves there with him, she can enroll at one of these colleges.

I felt better when I heard she could continue her education. But I'm still sad that she's gone back to Pakistan. Being in different high schools was OK, because we could at least see each other on weekends, but living in different countries bugs me a lot.

I called her recently, after she'd been in Pakistan for three weeks. To my relief, she sounded happy. She said that she has a kind husband, her in-laws are polite, and she has been admitted to a college where she'll be studying law. Her whole family has returned to Pakistan to live, too.

She seems content now with the way things worked out, but before she left for Pakistan, we talked about how we would treat our own daughters.

"If I have daughters I will never let them get married so soon," Nadira said. "I will let them finish their whole education first and then get married."

Sadia was 17 when she wrote this story.

Thinking for Myself in America

By Kanwal Javaid

One afternoon in my 9th grade class in Pakistan, my teacher started collecting our Arabic homework. I was nervous. For the very first time, I hadn't done the assignment. I went to my teacher and said politely, "Miss! I'm sorry, I didn't do my homework today."

She looked at me in surprise and roared, "Now you'll have to do your homework five times! Go stand by the wall and do it."

Every one of the 92 students in my class watched me as I stood by the wall, trying to do the work I'd copied from the blackboard into my scraggly notebook a day before. I was so embarrassed that I started crying. I worked like that for the full period in shame. Afterwards I began to wonder, "How is this helping to educate students?"

My punishment was lenient compared to things I saw growing up. In 8th grade, my teacher punished four students for murmuring while she was writing on the blackboard. She made them stand on their chairs for the next two periods with their arms raised straight up, while their entire bodies trembled from the strain. I saw other teachers punish students by beating them with rods.

This was common in Pakistani schools. Supposedly, it taught students to be organized and prepared, but I felt it only discouraged us. I also felt bored and disconnected from what I was learning. If somebody had asked me what I was good at, I wouldn't have been able to answer. Though I was doing well in every subject, I didn't care about any of it. Sometimes the only reason I paid attention was because I was scared I'd get hit by the teacher if I didn't.

In Pakistan, we were punished for talking to classmates. Here we were actually required to converse with them.

And the teachers could never provide students with individual attention, because the average class had 70 students. By the time I was in high school, I was fed up with school in Pakistan.

Then, when I was 16, my family moved to New York City. My father had been here for more than four years and I was happy to see him. We spent the summer just looking through the windows of the shops in Manhattan and walking around our new neighborhood in Queens.

One day in August, one of my father's Pakistani colleagues, Ghazala (not her real name), came to our house to visit. "You'll really enjoy your high school," she told me. She said that schools in the U.S. were friendly, teachers were affectionate, and classes were small.

"When can we go?" I asked her. I was excited to see everything she'd told me about. Finally, about a week later, Ghazala took my sister and me to register at one of New York's international high schools for new immigrant teens. On September 8th, I started my first day of school in the U.S.

Even though Ghazala had given me an idea of what the school would be like, I was so nervous my legs wouldn't stop trembling. In Pakistan, on a newcomer's first day of school, all the other students play pranks. They'll splash water on her shirt, or point her toward the bathroom instead of her classroom.

But from the beginning, I saw that school really was different in this country. When I peered into room MB48, where I was supposed to go, I was excited to see that it was small. In Pakistan, the classrooms are huge and filled with too many students.

My guidance counselor took me inside and introduced me to the teachers and students. I got my free Metrocard, a pass that allows me to use all the city's subways and buses, and this was like a fantasy because in Pakistan we had to pay for our transportation. Here it felt like the school was paying me to study. I watched students walking around, chatting with each other and talking frankly with teachers. I'd never imagined school could be like this.

My English teacher gave us assignments to discuss and work on with our classmates. Unlike in Pakistan, where we were punished for talking to classmates, here we were actually required to converse with them.

One day, my English teacher was talking about our poetry project. I was listening quietly, as usual. Suddenly he said, "Kanwal, what do you think is Shakespeare's point of view in this poem?"

I was speechless. It was the first time a teacher had asked for my opinion. At first, I didn't know what my opinion was, because I'd never really thought for myself before. But he encouraged me to just say whatever I thought.

He asked me the same question in different ways to help me think. "OK, what's the main idea of this poem?" he asked. Then, "Tell me the similes and metaphors used for the woman in this poem." He made me feel free to answer the question, so I told him how I thought Shakespeare was using metaphors to create a lively picture of what the woman looked like.

As I began to share my thoughts and ideas with the class in the weeks that followed, I started to learn that at my new school, being a good student wasn't about being obedient and quiet like in Pakistan. It was about developing your curiosity to learn new things.

In November, my history class had to do a project based on a made-up court case. The case was about a newspaper that published an article about a secret laboratory where the government made explosives. The court was arguing whether the newspaper should be allowed to tell the government's secrets.

Our class was divided into groups consisting of lawyers and judges. I was a lawyer defending the newspaper. On the day of the case, we all dressed up like lawyers and judges. The judges came into class and we all stood up. Our chief justice ordered us to sit down and start our arguments.

At first, I didn't know what my opinion was, because I'd never really thought for myself before.

The government's lawyers argued that the secret laboratory was making explosives to protect people, and that the newspaper should have kept it a secret. "Your Honor, the government has a right to change rules and regulations to keep people safe," they said.

Then it was our turn. I had prepared my arguments using the Constitution and previous court cases as a reference. I stood up and said, "Your Honor, the First Amendment clearly states that the press has the freedom to publish whatever they want. Our readers have a right to know that this lab has dangerous effects on the environment."

As I delivered my arguments, I felt like I could do anything. Everyone was interested in what we were saying and our group won the case because of our preparation and our passion.

This project made me feel confident for the first time in my life. I wondered why teachers in Pakistan didn't do these kinds of creative projects in classes. It taught us public speaking skills, responsibility, and critical thinking. And it helped create an atmosphere of politeness and encouragement.

Now I'm almost finished with my first year in an American school, and I see how much I've changed in such a short time. The tough discipline in Pakistan did make me a good and punctual student. But I wasn't interested in anything. After the months I've spent here, I'm eager to learn about current affairs, politics, and music.

I think we can create a better society by educating students through affection and care than we can using intimidation and punishment. Students are the future pillars of the country, and if those pillars aren't strong, the whole structure of the country may fall down. The best way to make students strong is to encourage their curiosity and build their confidence.

I feel more sure of myself and my decisions than I did a year ago, and I feel courageous and alive when I participate in class or have conversations with my teachers about the world around us. Before this year, I never thought about possible careers. Now I see there are many choices for me and I feel confident and excited about my future.

Kanwal was 17 when she wrote this story. She went on to attend Queens College, majoring in accounting.

Carla Chacon

Rookie Mistake

By Mohammed Hussain

Gym was about to begin. We 8th grade boys sat in rows brimming with the blues, greens, oranges, and reds of our gym clothes. Suddenly our loud banter turned into a silent murmur. Mr. O'Hara, the gym teacher, was speaking.

"Basketball tryouts will take place after school today in the gym," he announced.

I looked at the other boys and could see the excitement on their faces. Making the basketball team would be a dream come true: You'd get to play one of the greatest sports in America while having the honor of representing the school. Most importantly, you'd gain popularity, and with popularity came something else: girls. Few boys in that gym class would give up a chance to get popular with females.

All of this meant that the competition at tryouts would be fierce, but I loved competition and I wanted to be a part of the excitement. Even though I was rather short for my age, and couldn't play basketball well, by the end of the day, my mind was set. I would try out—even if it meant staying after school without my parents' permission.

Attending basketball tryouts would be better than going home. Home was the dungeon where my three little sisters outnumbered me. Any time I tried to watch my favorite TV shows, they changed the channel. Whenever I went on the computer, they'd ask me to show them episodes of the Simpsons. If I said no, they'd stay right there, giving me no chance to enjoy surfing the Internet alone.

And if I got annoyed and tried to hit one of my sisters, they'd all fight back: pulling my hair, throwing me on the ground, and punching me relentlessly. To top it all off, when my mother came to see what the commotion was, I was the one who'd get in trouble because I was older.

I also knew that at home, I'd have to deal with my mother's constant shouting to clean the dishes and not stay on the computer for long. My whole family is Bengali and we're the first of our lineage to live in America. Though my parents and grandmother came to this country to chase the American dream, they never chased Western ideals. They brought their rigid standards with them, and expected me to be devoted to my Muslim religion, my family, and my education. They expected me to spend less time on the computer than I wanted and generally obey their commands.

Although I was born in Bangladesh, I came to America at a young age. I feel more American than Bengali because I've grown up around this society and its more lax nature. But I've never felt completely free to enjoy this laxity because of my family. I used to imagine what it would like to be a typical American teenager, the youth who did whatever he wanted—going home late, always hanging out with friends, indulging in materialistic desires.

This idea was in my head when I decided to stay for basketball tryouts. Just for today, I thought, I want to be away from my mother's constant pestering. Just for today, I want independence.

I was fairly sure that staying after school for academic reasons would be acceptable to my parents, but staying for basketball would be out of the question. So I made up a lie to tell my mother: I would say I fell asleep on the bus and missed my stop. This lie would keep me from getting into trouble when I finally did get home. Reassured, I decided it was time to have fun playing basketball.

After school, I went into the gym for tryouts as I had planned. I left my jacket on the benches with my book bag and went to stand in line with the other boys. For a moment, my eyes turned to the direction of the window. I saw the gloomy, gray sky. I could sense the approaching rain and the dark, ominous clouds; it gave me a queasy feeling and seemed to foreshadow something bad. Guilt was creeping up on me; I knew I shouldn't be here, and I knew that lying to my mother about why I was late was immoral.

As those boys and I stood straight as soldiers, I felt powerful: I belonged here with them.

But as all those boys and I stood straight as soldiers, I felt powerful: I belonged here with them. I had the feeling you only get when you're with people who truly know you. In my home, I couldn't find that feeling: my mom seemed to want to mold me into a perfect boy, and my younger sisters just thought about what they wanted. No one at home asked me about my day; no one bothered to try to understand my life.

My peers, however, shared the same goals. We all wanted to compete and have a good time. Each of us understood the others' feelings. Knowing this made me feel a mixture of power and confidence, as a person may feel before he sets out to accomplish a task that he knows he can fulfill.

Mr. O'Hara told us to do some general exercises—like running around the gym—and gave us tests that measured our basketball abilities, like shooting the ball while moving through an obstacle course. I wasn't any good, but I was having so much fun. Even if I missed shots or bumped into other students, it was great to be away from the responsibilities of home.

Even as I enjoyed myself, I wondered if I'd made a mistake by not notifying my mother. She had the right to know where I was. Still, I thought, she didn't have the right to boss me around all the time. It was really her fault, I rationalized, that I hadn't called. After all, if she didn't make me go through hell with all those chores, I wouldn't have to stay away to escape the madness.

Suddenly, late into the tryouts, I heard an announcement over the loudspeaker calling for one Mohammed Hussain to go down into the main office. I suddenly realized it was me they were calling. Once again, I had a queasy feeling. I had never before been called to the office. My footsteps made an eerie noise as I ran out of the gym and through the deserted halls. My hands were numb and my heart beat rapidly. Time seemed to have stopped.

I had a feeling I had been called because my parents were looking for me. They would find out I had acted selfishly and foolishly, which would mean punishment. I hoped that my mistake didn't result in fewer freedoms at home: no more Playstation 2 or going on the computer.

But when I got to the main office, Playstation slipped from my mind entirely. There was my mother in her black coat, her embroidered scarlet scarf on her head. My older sister, Farzana, stood next to her. I had expected anger, but what surprised me were the tears on my mother's face.

Her face had blotches of red, and those tears were carrying away what little mascara she wore. The way she looked at me—

with a mixture of agony, relief, and joy—knocked some sense into me.

"Mom, Mom, what is wrong?" I asked her in Bengali. She hugged me tightly, as a blind man would hold a strand of light, but said nothing. Then Farzana looked at me in her usual, chastising way—like I was a two-year-old who was caught with his hand in the candy jar—and said: "I told her, 'He's probably at school doing something,' but she wouldn't listen. She thought you'd been kidnapped."

"Mom, what is wrong?" I asked. She hugged me tightly, as a blind man would hold a strand of light.

I couldn't believe what I was hearing. The outlandishness of what had gone through my mother's mind would have brought me to laughter in another situation, but not now. As I held my mother tightly, as though I was the parent and she was the baby, tears for the pain I had caused her began to flow freely from my eyes, too.

I felt like a miserable, worthless child—I had left my mother to suffer for the sake of my own selfish pleasure. Sharp knives of guilt cut through me. I didn't think about it at that moment, but maybe the reason I felt my mother's pain so much was that I had once felt the same worry about her, a few years before.

During New York's blackout in August of 2003, my sisters, grandmother, and I were at home when, suddenly, the television turned off and all the power went out in our building. As the evening wore on, my sisters and I sat on our heater by the window, watching night fall. Darkness came, and my sense of worry grew: Many people's parents had come home, but mine had not. I was 10 years old and terrified at the thought of losing my parents—so terrified, in fact, that I began to believe they had died in an accident, unable to see in the pitch darkness of that night.

Now I had grown older and become so wrapped up in my own life that it had never occurred to me that my parents might be worried in the same way about me. When I saw my mother the day of the tryouts, I realized how stupid I had been. I was thinking so much about me—my pains because of my mother's nagging—that I had forgotten what it's like to care about a loved one's safety.

I had also overlooked an important fact: my mother loves me. Her nagging is a sign of caring; because she wants me to become a better person, she makes me do the chores and limits my time on the computer.

Since that day, I've approached my family life differently. Whenever I get frustrated by constraints in my life or by my sisters' pestering, I remember that day and how lucky I am to have a family. I may crave certain freedoms that American teens have, but I've also seen how freedom can cause problems. I have friend who has become addicted to drugs and sex; he is not even 18 years old yet. When I think about him, I'm grateful for that watchfulness I get at home. Maybe he could have avoided the wrong path if someone had watched him closely like my parents watch me.

I'm now a high school junior, and I've matured. I'm older, taller, and smarter. My voice has deepened and a few months ago, I shaved for the first time.

My relationship with my parents has developed, too. They are still protective of me; when I began my internship last summer, they accompanied me to the office in Manhattan to make sure I found my way. Furthermore, I'm still expected to do chores and limit my computer time (although they've been less strict about these expectations).

But my parents realize I'm getting older, and they know age brings a greater degree of freedom. They let me hang out with friends now, because they trust that I will take care of myself. Staying late after school is not a problem anymore, so long as I let my parents know ahead of time.

And as they've learned to respect my need for greater freedom, I've learned to appreciate my parents' excessive care. I know my parents' strictness has taught me good morals and proper behavior, which will make me more independent and responsible in the long run. Had my parents not been so strict, I might not have learned how to take good care of myself.

Mohammad was 15 when he wrote this story.

Teens:
How to Get More Out of This Book

Self-help: The teens who wrote the stories in this book did so because they hope that telling their stories will help readers who are facing similar challenges. They want you to know that you are not alone, and that taking specific steps can help you manage or overcome very difficult situations. They've done their best to be clear about the actions that worked for them so you can see if they'll work for you.

Writing: You can also use the book to improve your writing skills. Each teen in this book wrote 5-10 drafts of his or her story before it was published. If you read the stories closely you'll see that the teens work to include a beginning, a middle, and an end, and good scenes, description, dialogue, and anecdotes (little stories). To improve your writing, take a look at how these writers construct their stories. Try some of their techniques in your own writing.

Resources on the Web

We will occasionally post Think About It questions on our website, www.youthcomm.org, to accompany stories in this and other Youth Communication books. We try out the questions with teens and post the ones they like best. Many teens report that writing answers to those questions in a journal is very helpful.

How to Use This Book in Staff Training

Staff say that reading these stories gives them greater insight into what teens are thinking and feeling, and new strategies for working with them. You can help the staff you work with by using these stories as case studies.

Select one story to read in the group, and ask staff to identify and discuss the main issue facing the teen. There may be disagreement about this, based on the background and experience of staff. That is fine. One point of the exercise is that teens have complex lives and needs. Adults can probably be more effective if they don't focus too narrowly and can see several dimensions of their clients.

Ask staff: What issues or feelings does the story provoke in them? What kind of help do they think the teen wants? What interventions are likely to be most promising? Least effective? Why? How would you build trust with the teen writer? How have other adults failed the teen, and how might that affect his or her willingness to accept help? What other resources would be helpful to this teen, such as peer support, a mentor, counseling, family therapy, etc?

Resources on the Web

From time to time we will post Think About It questions on our website, www.youthcomm.org, to accompany stories in this and other Youth Communication books. We try out the questions with teens and post the ones that they find most effective. We'll also post lessons for some of the stories. Adults can use the questions and lessons in workshops.

Discussion Guide

Teachers and Staff: How to Use This Book in Groups

When working with teens individually or in groups, you can use these stories to help young people face difficult issues in a way that feels safe to them. That's because talking about the issues in the stories usually feels safer to teens than talking about those same issues in their own lives. Addressing issues through the stories allows for some personal distance; they hit close to home, but not too close. Talking about them opens up a safe place for reflection. As teens gain confidence talking about the issues in the stories, they usually become more comfortable talking about those issues in their own lives.

Below are general questions to guide your discussion. In most cases you can read a story and conduct a discussion in one 45-minute session. Teens are usually happy to read the stories aloud, with each teen reading a paragraph or two. (Allow teens to pass if they don't want to read.) It takes 10-15 minutes to read a story straight through. However, it is often more effective to let workshop participants make comments and discuss the story as you go along. The workshop leader may even want to annotate her copy of the story beforehand with key questions.

If teens read the story ahead of time or silently, it's good to break the ice with a few questions that get everyone on the same page: Who is the main character? How old is she? What happened to her? How did she respond? Another good starting question is: "What stood out for you in the story?" Go around the room and let each person briefly mention one thing.

Then move on to open-ended questions, which encourage participants to think more deeply about what the writers were feeling, the choices they faced, and the actions they took. There are no right or wrong answers to the open-ended questions.

Open-ended questions encourage participants to think about how the themes, emotions, and choices in the stories relate to their own lives. Here are some examples of open-ended questions that we have found to be effective. You can use variations of these questions with almost any story in this book.

—What main problem or challenge did the writer face?

—What choices did the teen have in trying to deal with the problem?

—Which way of dealing with the problem was most effective for the teen? Why?

—What strengths, skills, or resources did the teen use to address the challenge?

—If you were in the writer's shoes, what would you have done?

—What could adults have done better to help this young person?

—What have you learned by reading this story that you didn't know before?

—What, if anything, will you do differently after reading this story?

—What surprised you in this story?

—Do you have a different view of this issue, or see a different way of dealing with it, after reading this story? Why or why not?

Credits

The stories in this book originally appeared in the following Youth Communication publications:

"Holding On to Who I Am," by Zaineb Nadeem, *New Youth Connections*, May/June 2004; "Jidda's Strength, Courage, and Wisdom," by Sara Said, *New Youth Connections*, November 2002; "My Love Affair With Indie Music," by Isma Aslam, *New Youth Connections*, November 2007; "Living Single: As a Muslim, I Don't Date," by Abanty Farzana, *New Youth Connections*, January/February 2002; "Where's Your Bomb?" by Mohamad Bazzi, *New Youth Connections*, January/February 1993; "Showing My Faith on the Outside," by Maria Zaman, *New Youth Connections*, September/October, 2004; "Why the Hijab?" by Maria Zaman, *New Youth Connections*, September/October 2004; "I'm American First," by Zeba A. Khann, *New Youth Connections*, November 1991; "Looking Over My Shoulder," by Abanty Farzana, *New Youth Connections*, November 2001; "Walking While Arab," by Sara Said, *New Youth Connections*, April 2002; "Singled Out," by Sabah Kaid Aljahmee, *New Youth Connections*, May/June 2003; "Getting My Green Card," by Fekri Kram, *Represent*, Winter 2010; "Land of Conflict," by Sara Said, *New Youth Connections*, May/June 2002; "No Place to Call Home," by Mohammad Ali, *New Youth Connections*, April 2000; "Not My Father's Daughter," by Sarvenaz Ezzati, *New Youth Connections*, September/October 1993; "University of Kitchen?" by Orubba Almansouri, *New Youth Connections*, March 2009; "Forced to Marry Young," by Sadia Jahangir, *New Youth Connections*, May/June 2004; "Thinking for Myself in America," by Kanwal Javaid, *New Youth Connections*, May/June 2006; "Rookie Mistake," by Mohammed Hussain, *New Youth Connections*, December-January 2009-2010.

About Youth Communication

Youth Communication, founded in 1980, is a nonprofit youth development program located in New York City whose mission is to teach writing, journalism, and leadership skills. The teenagers we train become writers for our websites and books and for two print magazines: *New Youth Connections*, a general-interest youth magazine, and *Represent*, a magazine by and for young people in foster care.

Each year, up to 100 young people participate in Youth Communication's school-year and summer journalism workshops, where they work under the direction of full-time professional editors. Most are African-American, Latino, or Asian, and many are recent immigrants. The opportunity to reach their peers with accurate portrayals of their lives and important self-help information motivates the young writers to create powerful stories.

Our goal is to run a strong youth development program in which teens produce high quality stories that inform and inspire their peers. Doing so requires us to be sensitive to the complicated lives and emotions of the teen participants while also providing an intellectually rigorous experience. We achieve that goal in the writing/teaching/editing relationship, which is the core of our program.

Our teaching and editorial process begins with discussions

between adult editors and the teen staff. In those meetings, the teens and the editors work together to identify the most important issues in the teens' lives and to figure out how those issues can be turned into stories that will resonate with teen readers.

Once story topics are chosen, students begin the process of crafting their stories. For a personal story, that means revisiting events in one's past to understand their significance for the future. For a commentary, it means developing a logical and persuasive point of view. For a reported story, it means gathering information through research and interviews. Students look inward and outward as they try to make sense of their experiences and the world around them and find the points of intersection between personal and social concerns. That process can take a few weeks or a few months. Stories frequently go through 10 or more drafts as students work under the guidance of their editors, the way any professional writer does.

Many of the students who walk through our doors have uneven skills, as a result of poor education, living under extremely stressful conditions, or coming from homes where English is a second language. Yet, to complete their stories, students must successfully perform a wide range of activities, including writing and rewriting, reading, discussion, reflection, research, interviewing, and typing. They must work as members of a team and they must accept individual responsibility. They learn to provide constructive criticism, and to accept it. They engage in explorations of truthfulness, fairness, and accuracy. They meet deadlines. They must develop the audacity to believe that they have something important to say and the humility to recognize that saying it well is not a process of instant gratification. Rather, it usually requires a long, hard struggle through many discussions and much rewriting.

It would be impossible to teach these skills and dispositions as separate, disconnected topics, like grammar, ethics, or assertiveness. However, we find that students make rapid progress when they are learning skills in the context of an inquiry that is personally significant to them and that will benefit their peers.

When teens publish their stories—in *New Youth Connections* and *Represent*, on the Web, and in other publications—they reach tens of thousands of teen and adult readers. Teachers, counselors, social workers, and other adults circulate the stories to young people in their classes and out-of-school youth programs. Adults tell us that teens in their programs—including many who are ordinarily resistant to reading—clamor for the stories. Teen readers report that the stories give them information they can't get anywhere else, and inspire them to reflect on their lives and open lines of communication with adults.

Writers usually participate in our program for one semester, though some stay much longer. Years later, many of them report that working here was a turning point in their lives—that it helped them acquire the confidence and skills that they needed for success in college and careers. Scores of our graduates have overcome tremendous obstacles to become journalists, writers, and novelists. They include National Book Award finalist and MacArthur Fellowship winner Edwidge Danticat, novelist Ernesto Quiñonez, writer Veronica Chambers, and *New York Times* reporter Rachel Swarns. Hundreds more are working in law, business, and other careers. Many are teachers, principals, and youth workers, and several have started nonprofit youth programs themselves and work as mentors—helping another generation of young people develop their skills and find their voices.

Youth Communication is a nonprofit educational corporation. Contributions are gratefully accepted and are tax deductible to the fullest extent of the law.

To make a contribution, or for information about our publications and programs, including our catalog of over 100 books and curricula for hard-to-reach teens, see www.youthcomm.org.

About the Editors

Marie Glancy O'Shea is is the editor of *New Youth Connections,* Youth Communication's magazine by and for New York City teens. Before joining Youth Communication in 2008, she worked for several years in print, radio, and online journalism in Dublin, Ireland, and in New York. As an undergraduate she received a Harper's Magazine Scholarship from the Overseas Press Club Foundation. She has a BA in English from Williams College, an M Phil in Anglo-Irish literature from Trinity College Dublin, and an MS in journalism from Columbia University.

Keith Hefner co-founded Youth Communication in 1980 and has directed it ever since. He is the recipient of the Luther P. Jackson Education Award from the New York Association of Black Journalists and a MacArthur Fellowship. He was also a Revson Fellow at Columbia University.

Laura Longhine is the editorial director at Youth Communication. She edited *Represent,* Youth Communication's magazine by and for youth in foster care, for three years, and has written for a variety of publications. She has a BA in English from Tufts University and an MS in Journalism from Columbia University.

More Helpful Books From Youth Communication

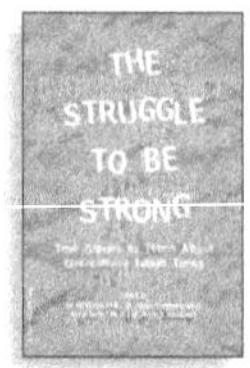

The Struggle to Be Strong: True Stories by Teens About Overcoming Tough Times. Foreword by Veronica Chambers. Help young people identify and build on their own strengths with 30 personal stories about resiliency. (Free Spirit)

Starting With "I": Personal Stories by Teenagers. "Who am I and who do I want to become?" Thirty-five stories examine this question through the lens of race, ethnicity, gender, sexuality, family, and more. Increase this book's value with the free Teacher's Guide, available from youthcomm.org. (Youth Communication)

Real Stories, Real Teens. Inspire teens to read and recognize their strengths with this collection of 26 true stories by teens. The young writers describe how they overcame significant challenges and stayed true to themselves. Also includes the first chapters from three novels in the Bluford Series. (Youth Communication)

The Courage to Be Yourself: True Stories by Teens About Cliques, Conflicts, and Overcoming Peer Pressure. In 26 first-person stories, teens write about their lives with searing honesty. These stories will inspire young readers to reflect on their own lives, work through their problems, and help them discover who they really are. (Free Spirit)

Out With It: Gay and Straight Teens Write About Homosexuality. Break stereotypes and provide support with this unflinching look at gay life from a teen's perspective. With a focus on urban youth, this book also includes several heterosexual teens' transformative experiences with gay peers. (Youth Communication)

Things Get Hectic: Teens Write About the Violence That Surrounds Them. Violence is commonplace in many teens' lives, be it bullying, gangs, dating, or family relationships. Hear the experiences of victims, perpetrators, and witnesses through more than 50 real-world stories. (Youth Communication)

From Dropout to Achiever: Teens Write About School. Help teens overcome the challenges of graduating, which may involve overcoming family problems, bouncing back from a bad semester, or even dropping out for a time. These teens show how they achieve academic success. (Youth Communication)

American Me: Teens Write About the Immigrant Experience. Help both foreign- and native-born teens understand the conflicts and contradictions of the immigrant experience. Teens from around the world describe the exciting (and scary) experience of leaving their countries and coming to the U.S. (Youth Communication)

Sticks and Stones: Teens Write About Bullying. Shed light on bullying, as told from the perspectives of the bully, the victim, and the witness. These stories show why bullying occurs, the harm it causes, and how it might be prevented. (Youth Communication)

Boys to Men: Teens Write About Becoming a Man. The young men in this book write about confronting the challenges of growing up. Their honesty and courage make them role models for teens who are bombarded with contradictory messages about what it means to be a man. (Youth Communication)

Through Thick and Thin: Teens Write About Obesity, Eating Disorders, and Self Image. Help teens who struggle with obesity, eating disorders, and body weight issues. These stories show the pressures teens face when they are confronted by unrealistic standards for physical appearance, and how emotions can affect the way we eat. (Youth Communication)

To order these and other books, go to:
www.youthcomm.org
or call 212-279-0708 x115

www.ingramcontent.com/pod-product-compliance
Lightning Source LLC
LaVergne TN
LVHW010105110826
845155LV00028B/487